The Mathematics of Borrowing
Mathematics for Everyday Living

Roland E. Larson
Robert P. Hostetler

Exercises prepared with the assistance of
David E. Heyd

Updated and revised by
Marjorie J. Bertram

meridian
CREATIVE GROUP

A DIVISION OF LARSON TEXTS, INC.

This book is published by
Meridian Creative Group, a Division of Larson Texts, Inc.

Please address all correspondence to:
Home School Division
Meridian Creative Group
5178 Station Road
Erie, PA 16510
(800) 530-2355
http://www.home.meridiancg.com

Trademark acknowledgement:
Explorer Plus is a trademark of Texas Instruments Incorporated

Printed in the United States of America

International Standard Book Number: ISBN 1-887050-27-2

10 9 8 7 6 5 4 3 2 1

Preface

Mathematics for Everyday Living is a series of workbooks designed to give students a solid and practical grasp of the mathematics used in daily life.

Each workbook in the series features practical consumer information, solved examples, and "Try one!" exercises with which students can use a particular skill immediately following its introduction. Complete solutions to the "Try one!" exercises are provided in the back of the workbook along with answers to odd-numbered exercises.

The workbook, *"The Mathematics of Borrowing,"* is divided into six sections, each of which address a set of mathematical skills and concepts involved in the borrowing of money.

- The first section, "Promissory Notes," shows the way in which lenders calculate the cost of borrowing money for a fixed period of time, paying it back in one lump sum.

- Section two, "Installment Loans," shows students how to amortize a loan over time, determine the monthly payments, and calculate the finance charge.

- In the third section, "Financing a New Car," the student will learn how to figure out monthly car payments and the balance due on a car loan upon its resale.

- In section four, "Home Mortgages," the student will gain insight as to exactly how much interest is paid over a long-term installment loan such as a mortgage.

- Section five, "Credit Cards," teaches the student the variety of ways in which credit card companies calculate the monthly finance charge on outstanding balances.

- Finally, section six features a spotlight on a career as a Credit Clerk. Educational requirements, job descriptions and employment outlook are all addressed.

Finally, a "Thank-you" is owed to Richard Bertram for his patience and support, Steve Kifer for his technical assistance, and Cheryl Bernik for her help in organizing this project.

Marjorie J. Bertram

Contents

Section 1
Promissory Notes

Most of us have borrowed money on some occasion. In years past, consumers tended to restrict their borrowing to major purchases such as a home, a car, or a new business. However, in recent years, the reasons for borrowing money have become so numerous that most consumers consider borrowing a routine part of their lives. For example, it is common to obtain loans for college tuition, vacations, sailboats, dental work, holiday gift giving, or furniture.

At the time you obtain a loan, you are expected to sign a **promissory note** in which you promise to repay the loan within a certain period of time. This time period is called the **term** of the loan. Figure 1 shows an example of a promissory note.

Figure 1

No. 2786   Boise, Idaho, May 10   19 96 $ 1240.00

_____ninety days_____ *after date the undersigned (jointly and severally if more than one) promise(s) to pay to the order of* _____First National Bank_____

_____One thousand two hundred forty and no/100_____ *Dollars*

Payable at _____First National Bank, Boise Idaho_____

Each and every party to this instrument, either as maker, endorser, surety or otherwise, hereby waives demand, notice, protest, and all other demands and notices and assents to any extension of the time of payment or any other indulgence, to any substitution, exchange or release of collateral and/or to the release of any other party.

Address _____174 Maple Avenue_____   *Signed* Jane Doe

Only _____Boise, Idaho_____   *By* _____

The amount actually received in a loan is called the **loan proceeds** and the total amount the borrower must pay the lender is called the **total payment** or **total amount due**. For example, the total amount due for the loan illustrated in Figure 1 is $1240.00.

The ability of a person to obtain a loan is called **credit**. If you have good credit, you can obtain a loan more readily than if your credit is poor or unestablished. Credit costs money. When you obtain a loan, you are borrowing someone else's money and you must (normally) pay to do this. The **cost of credit** for a particular loan is defined as the difference between the total amount due and the loan proceeds. Thus, the cost of credit, the total amount due, and the loan proceeds are related by the equation

Cost of Credit = Total Amount Due − Loan Proceeds.

EXAMPLE 1 **Finding the total amount due and the cost of credit**

Karen and Ron Sinclair purchase a refrigerator for $950.89 plus a 6% sales tax. The appliance store has a one-year loan program which allows the Sinclairs to pay for the refrigerator by making twelve equal monthly payments of $95.75. Find the cost of credit for this loan.

SOLUTION

Since there are twelve equal payments of $95.75, the total amount due for this loan is

Total Amount Due = (12)($95.75) = $1149.00.

The loan proceeds are found by adding the cost of the refrigerator to the 6% sales tax:

Loan Proceeds = $950.89 + ($950.89)(0.06)

$\approx$ $950.89 + $57.05

= $1007.94.

Finally, the cost of credit for this loan is

Cost of Credit = Total Amount Due − Loan Proceeds

= $1149.00 − $1007.94

= $141.06. ◆

Try one!

Robert and Sandra Dunlop purchase a computer at an electronics store. The price of the computer is $1599.99 plus 6% sales tax. Sandra's parents lend them the money to buy the computer and ask them to pay it back in two years by making 24 equal payments of $74.20. Find the cost of credit for this loan.

Answer: _____

Private loans from friends or relatives such as the one in the first Try one! can be very beneficial to both lender and borrower. However, on occasion, misunderstandings concerning the loan can cause serious problems. The mutual understanding of the exact obligations involved in a loan is even more critical when dealing with lending institutions. To help borrowers understand the contractual obligations of a particular loan, the federal government requires lending institutions to disclose to each borrower *in writing* several pertinent facts regarding the loan *before* the borrower is asked to sign a promissory note. This requirement is called the **Truth-In-Lending Law**. The basic features of a Truth-In-Lending Law disclosure are shown in Table 1.

T A B L E 1	DISCLOSURES REQUIRED BY FEDERAL TRUTH-IN-LENDING LAW

Loan Proceeds	Other Charges	Amount Financed	Finance Charge	Total Amount	Annual Percentage Rate	Payable in one payment.
$ _____	$ _____	$ _____	$ _____	$ _____	_____ %	_____ on demand
						_____ on _____ 19 _____

As can be seen in Table 1, the Truth-In-Lending Law requires lending institutions to classify the cost of credit of every loan into two categories:

1. **Finance charges** such as interest, carrying charges, and service charges, and

2. **Other charges** such as insurance premiums, investigation of credit fees, and filing fees.

Although the "other charges" may be paid at the time of the loan, they are normally incorporated into the loan and together with the loan proceeds they make up the **amount financed**, or the principal. The loan proceeds, other charges, amount financed, finance charge, and total amount due are related in the following way.

Total Amount Due

$$= \text{Loan Proceeds} + \text{Cost of Credit}$$

$$= \text{Loan Proceeds} + (\text{Other Charges} + \text{Finance Charge})$$

$$= (\text{Loan Proceeds} + \text{Other Charges}) + \text{Finance Charge}$$

$$= \text{Amount Financed} + \text{Finance Charge}$$

Thus, if we let

$A = $ total amount due

$P = $ amount financed (principal) and

$F = $ finance charge,

we have

$$A = P + F.$$

EXAMPLE 2	**Finding the amount financed and the total amount due**

Ralph Taylor purchases a new washer and dryer for $895.00 plus $53.70 sales tax. He pays $100.70 down and borrows the remaining $848.00 of the cost. As Ralph is signing the papers for the loan, he is presented with a Truth-In-Lending disclosure specifying the loan proceeds to be $848.00, the other charges to be $15.35 for life insurance and $34.60 for health and accident insurance, and the finance charge to be $215.17. What is the amount financed and what is the total amount due for this loan?

SOLUTION

The amount financed is

$$
\begin{array}{ll}
\$15.35 & \text{life insurance premium} \\
34.60 & \text{health and accident insurance premium} \\
\underline{+\ 848.00} & \text{loan proceeds} \\
\$897.95 & \text{amount financed.}
\end{array}
$$

The total amount due is

$$
\begin{array}{ll}
\$897.95 & \text{amount financed} \\
\underline{+\ 215.17} & \text{finance charge} \\
\$1113.12 & \text{total amount due.}
\end{array}
$$
◆

Try one!

Carl Bennett is setting up a car shop and buys equipment totalling $899.95 plus $49.50 sales tax. He pays $189.89 down and borrows the remaining $759.56. The Truth-In-Lending disclosure specifies the loan proceeds to be $759.56, the insurance charges to be $47.35, and the finance charge to be $197.46. What is the amount financed and what is the total amount due for this loan?

Amount Financed: _____   Total Due: _____

There are many sources of money available to the average borrower: small loan companies, credit unions, banks, insurance companies, family, friends, and the government. The cost of credit varies with the lending source and it is not unusual to find differences of as much as several hundred dollars in the cost of credit charged at different lending sources. In some favorable instances, the cost of credit may even be zero for all or part of the loan. For example, children may be able to obtain an interest-free loan from their parents and students may qualify for tuition loans in which the cost of credit is paid by the federal government until nine months after the student leaves school.

Repayment of a loan can occur in many ways. The most common way to repay a loan is by means of monthly payments. A detailed discussion of this type of repayment occurs in Section 2. A second type of repayment is by means of a single payment at the end of the term of the loan. This type of loan is called a **time note**. Common terms for such notes are 30 days, 60 days, 90 days, six months, one year, and 18 months.

EXAMPLE 3   **Finding the due date and the total amount due**

Mary Johnson is moving from Dallas to Pittsburgh. She wishes to sell her home in Dallas and use the money as a down payment on a home in Pittsburgh. Unfortunately, the moving date arrives before her Dallas home is sold so she decides to obtain a 90-day note from a Pittsburgh bank for $10,000.00. If the loan takes place on June 7, 1996 and her cost of credit includes $21.50 for the cost of the lien on the home, $244.27 for interest, and a $62.50 service charge, then when is the note due and how much is due at the end of 90 days?

SOLUTION

Since the loan occurred June 7, and is due 90 days from that time, we have

23	days remaining in June
31	days in July
31	days in August
+ 5	days in September
90	days.

Thus, the note is due on September 5, 1996. On September 5, the total amount due is

$10,000.00	loan proceeds
21.50	cost of lien on home
244.27	interest
+ 62.50	service charge
$10,328.27	total amount due.

◆

The one piece of information shown in a Truth-In-Lending Law disclosure (see Table 1) that we have not discussed is the **annual percentage rate**. *For a time note,* the annual percentage rate R and the finance charge F are related by the equation

$$F = PRT$$

where

$$T = \frac{\text{exact number of days}}{365} = \frac{D}{365}.$$

To solve the equation $F = PRT$ for R, we can divide both sides by PT to obtain

$$R = \frac{F}{PT}.$$

Calculator Hints

$$R = \frac{F}{PT} = \frac{F}{P\left(\frac{D}{365}\right)}$$

To find the annual percentage rate of a time note using your calculator, apply the following steps:

1. Divide D by 365.

2. Multiply by P.

3. Press the $\boxed{1/x}$ key and multiply by F.

4. Convert to percent by multiplying by 100.

EXAMPLE 4	Finding the annual percentage rate

In Example 3, Mary Johnson took out a 90-day note to cover the down payment on her new home while her old home was being sold. What is the annual percentage rate for this loan?

SOLUTION

Referring back to Example 3, we see that the amount financed is

$10,000.00	loan proceeds
+ 21.50	cost of lien on home
$10,021.50	amount financed.

Furthermore, the finance charge is

$244.27	interest
+ 62.50	service charge
$306.77	finance charge.

EXAMPLE 4

Steps	Display
90 ÷ 365 =	0.246575342
× 10,021.50 =	2471.054795
1/x × 306.77 =	0.124145365
× 100 =	12.41453652

Finally, since $T = \dfrac{90}{365}$, the annual percentage rate is

$$R = \frac{F}{PT} = \frac{\$306.77}{(\$10,021.50)\left(\frac{90}{365}\right)} \approx 12.41\%. \qquad \blacklozenge$$

Try one!

Mark Richards wants to restore an old car and sell it. He estimates that the restoration will cost $5000.00 and take less than three months to complete. He decides to obtain a 90-day note from the bank to cover the expense. If the loan takes place on April 6, 1996 and his cost of credit includes $117.12 for interest and a $30.00 service charge, when is the note due and how much is due at the end of 90 days?

Note Due Date: _____

Amount Due: _____

When shopping for a loan, it is important to compare annual percentage rates as shown *in writing* on a Truth-In-Lending Law declaration. Remember that the interest rate *quoted* by a lender (which we denote by r) may not be the same as the annual percentage rate. Differences between r and R stem from differences in the way the finance charge is calculated. Here are three common practices which yield a larger finance charge than that implied by the quoted interest rate.

1. The finance charge F may include additional service or carrying charges.

$$F = PrT + S$$

This practice is misleading since these additional charges are really disguised forms of interest and should be included in the quoted interest rate.

2. The finance charge F may be figured using **Banker's Rule**.

$$F = Prt = Pr\left(\frac{D}{360}\right)$$

Under this practice, a year is assumed to have 360 rather than 365 days. This makes for slightly larger finance charges since the fraction $t = \frac{D}{360}$ is slightly larger than $T = \frac{D}{365}$.

3. The finance charge F may be figured at a discounted rate.

$$F = ArT$$

This practice is blatantly unfair since it bases the finance charge on the total amount due rather than the amount received. Remember that $A = F + P$; thus, basing the finance charge on A rather than P means that the borrower is being charged interest on interest. In this case,

$$P = A - ArT = A(1 - rT).$$

EXAMPLE 5	**Finding the annual percentage rate with Banker's Rule**

The Hofstetter family is planning an extended vacation in Switzerland and wishes to borrow $2500.00 for 90 days. They are offered a loan at 12% interest calculated with *Banker's Rule*. What is the true annual percentage rate of this loan?

SOLUTION

If we let $r = 0.12$ and $t = \frac{90}{360}$, then the finance charge for 90 days is

$$F = Prt = (\$2500.00)(0.12)\left(\tfrac{90}{360}\right) = \$75.00.$$

Now, to find the annual percentage rate, we let $T = \frac{90}{365}$ and obtain

$$R = \frac{F}{PT} = \frac{\$75.00}{(\$2500.00)\left(\frac{90}{365}\right)} \approx 0.1217 = 12.17\%. \qquad \blacklozenge$$

Try one!

What is the true annual percentage rate for a loan of $3500.00 for 90 days at 13% interest calculated with Banker's Rule?

Answer: _____

Calculator Hints

$$F = A - P = \frac{P}{1 - rT} - P$$

To find the finance charge using a discounted rate using your calculator, apply the following steps:

1. Multiply r by T.

2. Change signs and add 1.

3. Press the ☐1/x key.

4. Multiply by P.*

5. Subtract P.

*Step 4 results in the total amount due, $A = \frac{P}{1 - rT}$.

Typically in a loan application, it is P that is known and A that is unknown. For this reason the formula for the finance charge

$$F = ArT$$

is not as useful as the comparable formula

$$F = A - P = \frac{P}{1 - rT} - P$$

where r is the *discounted rate*.

EXAMPLE 6   **Finding the annual percentage rate given the discounted rate**

Amy and Frank Wollard go to a bank to borrow $750.00 for 60 days. The loan officer at the bank tells them that the bank will charge them $14\frac{1}{2}\%$ interest at a *discounted rate*.

a. What is the finance charge for this loan?

b. What is the true annual percentage rate for this loan?

EXAMPLE 6a

Steps	Display
0.145 ☒ 60 ☐	8.7
☐ 365 ☐	0.023835616
☐+C☐ ☐ 1 ☐	0.976164384
☐1/x☐	1.024417626
☒ 750 ☐	768.3132192
☐ 750 ☐	18.3132192

SOLUTION

a. From the given information, we have $P = \$750.00$, $r = 0.145$, and $T = \frac{60}{365}$. Therefore, the finance charge is

$$F = \frac{P}{1 - rT} - P = \frac{\$750.00}{1 - (0.145)\left(\frac{60}{365}\right)} - \$750.00 \approx \$18.31.$$

b. The annual percentage rate for this loan is

$$R = \frac{F}{PT} = \frac{\$18.31}{(\$750.00)\left(\frac{60}{365}\right)} \approx 0.1485 = 14.85\%. \qquad \blacklozenge$$

Try one!

Robin and Brian Corbin go to a bank to borrow $950.00 for 60 days. The loan officer at the bank tells them that the bank will charge them $13\frac{3}{4}\%$ interest at a discounted rate. What is the finance charge for this loan? What is the true annual percentage rate for this loan?

Finance Charge: _____

Annual Percentage Rate: _____

Table 2 illustrates the discrepancies that can exist between the quoted interest rate and the *true* annual percentage rate.

TABLE 2   **QUOTED INTEREST RATE VERSUS THE ANNUAL PERCENTAGE RATE ($P = \$1000.00$, 180 days)**

	Quoted Rate	Finance Charge	Annual % Rate
Additional service charge of $7.50	$r = 15\%$	$F = PrT + S = (\$1000.00)(0.15)\left(\frac{180}{365}\right) + \$7.50 \approx \$81.47$	$R = \dfrac{F}{PT} \approx 16.5\%$
Banker's Rule	$r = 15\%$	$F = PrT = (\$1000.00)(0.15)\left(\frac{180}{360}\right) = \$75.00$	$R = \dfrac{F}{PT} \approx 15.2\%$
Discounted rate ($A = \$1079.88$)	$r = 15\%$	$F = ArT + S = (\$1079.88)(0.15)\left(\frac{180}{365}\right) \approx \$79.88$	$R = \dfrac{F}{PT} \approx 16.2\%$

When the term of a time note is given in months rather than days, the day (of the month) the loan is due coincides with the day (of the month) the loan was issued. Here are some examples.

Date of Loan	Term	Date Due
March 7, 1995	18 months	September 7, 1996
February 12, 1996	6 months	August 12, 1996
August 31, 1996	3 months	November 30, 1996*

*In the case of a loan made on August 31 for three months, the due date is November 30 since November has only 30 days.

EXAMPLE 7   Finding the finance charge given the term in months

Since the annual percentage rate of a time note is always based on the exact number of days in the term, the finance charge for a time note whose term is given in months depends upon the day of issue. To illustrate this, find the finance charge for a loan of $3500.00 for six months at an annual percentage rate of 18.75% if the loan is taken out on May 1, 1995.

SOLUTION

If the loan is taken out on May 1, 1995 for six months, then it would be due on November 1, 1995. The number of days between these two dates is

30	days remaining in May
30	days in June
31	days in July
31	days in August
30	days in September
31	days in October
+ 1	day in November
184	days.

Therefore, the time is $T = \frac{184}{365}$ and the finance charge is

$$F = PRT = (\$3500.00)(0.1875)\left(\tfrac{184}{365}\right) \approx \$330.82.$$ ◆

Try one!

Find the finance charge for a loan of $3500.00 for six months at an annual percentage rate of 18.75% if the loan is taken out on November 5, 1996.

Answer: _____

Important Terms

additional charges

A, total amount due

Banker's Rule

cost of credit

credit

D, number of days in term

discounted rate

F, finance charge

loan proceeds

other charges

P, amount financed

promissory note

R, annual percentage rate

r, quoted interest rate

S, service charge

t, term for Banker's rate

T, term of note

time note

Truth-In-Lending Law

Important Formulas

$$F = PRT$$

$$R = \frac{F}{PT} = \frac{F}{P\left(\frac{D}{365}\right)}$$

$$A = P + F$$

$$F = PrT + S \quad \text{(Additional Service charges)}$$

$$F = Prt = Pr\left(\frac{D}{360}\right) \quad \text{(Banker's Rule)}$$

$$F = ArT = \frac{P}{1 - rT} - P \quad \text{(Discounted Rate)}$$

CONSUMER HINTS

- The difference between the least expensive and the most expensive loan can amount to hundreds of dollars on major purchases. Comparison shopping is important. Federal law provides a means for getting the best loan. Do not neglect the advantages of such a law.

- In making comparisons between various lending sources, you need to know the following.
  1. The loan proceeds
  2. Other charges
  3. Amount financed
  4. Finance charges
  5. Annual percentage rate

SECTION 1   EXERCISES

1. Fill in the blanks in the following table. (Note: 1996 is a leap year.)

Date of Loan	Term	Date Due
July 19, 1995	3 months	_____
July 19, 1995	90 days	_____
_____	6 months	November 20, 1996
_____	180 days	November 20, 1996
January 13, 1995	_____	July 13, 1996
January 13, 1996	_____	April 12, 1996

2. Fill in the blanks in the following table. (Note: 1996 is a leap year.)

Date of Loan	Term	Date Due
_____	30 days	July 20, 1996
December 14, 1996	_____	February 12, 1997
November 18, 1995	180 days	_____
November 18, 1995	15 months	_____
_____	6 months	January 5, 1996
May 31, 1996	45 days	_____

3. Ralph Holzer purchases a mountain bike for $489.00 plus a 6% sales tax. He pays $75.00 down and finances the remainder of the cost.

    a. Determine the amount of sales tax.

                                                        Answer: _____

    b. Determine the loan proceeds.

                                                        Answer: _____

4. Amy Barnes' new nine-cycle washer cost $319.95 plus a 5% sales tax. She paid 25% (of her total bill) and financed the remainder for 60 days.

    a. Determine the amount of sales tax.

                                                        Answer: _____

    b. Determine the loan proceeds.

                                                        Answer: _____

5. For the purchase in Exercise 3, suppose that Ralph signed a 90-day promissory note.

    a. Determine the "other charges" if Ralph was required to pay an insurance premium equal to 2% of the loan proceeds.

Answer: _____

    b. Add the result of part (a) to the loan proceeds to determine the amount financed.

Answer: _____

    c. Determine the finance charge if the interest rate is 12% (annual percentage rate) of the amount financed.

Answer: _____

    d. Use the results of parts (a) and (c) to find the cost of credit of Ralph's loan.

Answer: _____

6. For the purchase in Exercise 4, suppose that Amy Barnes signed a 60-day promissory note.

   a. Determine the "other charges" if Amy was required to pay an insurance premium equal to 1% of the loan proceeds.

   Answer: _____

   b. Add the result of part (a) to the loan proceeds to determine the amount financed.

   Answer: _____

   c. Determine the finance charge if the interest rate is 18% (annual percentage rate) of the amount financed.

   Answer: _____

   d. Use the results of parts (a) and (c) to find the cost of credit of Amy's loan.

   Answer: _____

In Exercises 7–12, find the total amount due on each loan.

7. A loan of $800.00 for 90 days at an annual percentage rate of 18%.

Answer: _____

8. A loan of $1500.00 for 120 days at an annual percentage rate of 15%.

Answer: _____

9. A loan of $800.00 for three months at an annual percentage rate of 18%. (Assume the loan is taken out on June 1.)

Answer: _____

10. A loan of $1500.00 taken out on December 15, 1995 for six months at an annual percentage rate of 15%. (Recall that 1996 is a leap year.)

Answer: _____

11. A loan of $2000.00 taken out on June 1, 1995 for nine months at an annual percentage rate of 12%. (Recall that 1996 is a leap year.)

Answer: _____

12. A loan of $2500.00 taken out on September 15, 1994 for 180 days at an annual percentage rate of 18%.

Answer: _____

13. Bill and Carly Taylor took out a 90-day note for $1000.00. If the finance charge was $44.38, find the annual percentage rate of their loan.

Answer: _____

14. Margo Rossi took out a 60-day note for $800.00. If the finance charge was $19.73, find the annual percentage rate of Margo's loan.

Answer: _____

15. A furniture store advertises recliner chairs for $299.95 with no down payment. Bob Charters decides to buy one of the chairs and signs a 90-day note in which he agrees to pay the full amount plus interest calculated at 18% per year. If, in addition to the interest, Bob is asked to pay a $10.00 service charge, what is the actual annual percentage rate of his loan?

Answer: _____

16. A window air conditioner is on sale for $329.00. Suppose a customer purchases this air conditioner by paying $50.00 down with the remainder to be paid in 60 days. If the finance charge includes a 12% interest rate per year plus a $5.00 service charge, what is the actual annual percentage rate for the loan?

Answer: _____

17. A bank lends $500.00 to Carl Abernathy for one year at 12% interest (discounted rate).

a. Find the finance charge for this loan.

Answer: _____

b. What is the annual percentage rate for this loan?

Answer: _____

18. A bank lends $1500.00 to one of its customers for one year at $9\frac{1}{2}\%$ discounted interest.

   a. Find the finance charge for this loan.

                                 Answer: _____

   b. What is the annual percentage rate for this loan?

                                 Answer: _____

19. Determine the finance charge and the annual percentage rate on an $800.00 loan for 90 days at an annual discounted interest rate of 15%.

Finance Charge: _____   Annual Percentage Rate: _____

20. Determine the finance charge and the annual percentage rate on a $400.00 loan for 180 days at an annual discounted interest rate of 18%.

Finance Charge: _____   Annual Percentage Rate: _____

21. Mary Simmons borrows $10,000.00 for 90 days at 10% annual interest (Banker's Rule). What is the finance charge for this loan and what is the actual annual percentage rate?

Finance Charge: _____   Annual Percentage Rate: _____

22. Todd and Jean Cooper borrow $2500.00 for 120 days at $11\frac{1}{4}\%$ annual interest (Banker's Rule). What is the finance charge for this loan and what is the actual annual percentage rate?

Finance Charge: _____   Annual Percentage Rate: _____

Section 2

Installment Loans

In Section 1 we primarily discussed time notes for which the total amount due is paid in one payment at the end of the term of the loan. In this section we will focus on a more common way to repay a loan–by means of periodic payments or **installments**. This type of loan is called an **installment loan** and the payments usually occur monthly. The process of repaying an installment loan is called **amortization**.

Lending institutions normally determine the monthly payment for an installment loan from a table containing various interest rates and numbers of monthly installments. However, with a calculator, the average consumer can readily calculate monthly payments by means of the formula

$$M = P \left[\frac{\frac{R}{12}}{1 - \left(\frac{1}{\frac{R}{12} + 1} \right)^N} \right]$$

where

M = monthly payment,

P = amount financed (principal),

R = annual percentage rate,

and

N = number of monthly payments.

Calculator Hints

$$M = P \left[\frac{\frac{R}{12}}{1 - \left(\frac{1}{\frac{R}{12} + 1} \right)^N} \right]$$

To find the monthly payments for installment loans using your calculator, apply the following steps:

1. Divide R by 12 and store the result.

2. Add 1 and press the $\boxed{1/x}$ key.

3. Raise to the Nth power, change signs, and add 1.

4. Press the $\boxed{1/x}$ key

5. Multiply by memory.

6. Multiply by P.

7. Round to the nearest cent.

EXAMPLE 1   Finding monthly payments

Anthony Fonzo wishes to buy a jacuzzi bathtub for his newly remodeled bathroom. To do so he borrows $2800.00 that he plans to repay in 12 monthly payments. If the annual percentage rate is 10%, what is the monthly payment?

27

SOLUTION

EXAMPLE 1

Steps	Display
0.10 ÷ 12 =	0.008333333
STO	0.008333333
+ 1 =	1.008333333
1/x	0.991735537
yˣ 12 =	0.90521243
+⊂- + 1 =	0.09478757
1/x	10.54990647
× RCL =	0.087915887
× 2800 =	246.1644843

In this example, we have $P = \$2800.00$, $R = 0.10$, and $N = 12$. Therefore, the monthly payment is

$$M = P \left[\frac{\frac{R}{12}}{1 - \left(\frac{1}{\frac{R}{12} + 1}\right)^N} \right]$$

$$= (\$2800.00) \left[\frac{\frac{0.10}{12}}{1 - \left(\frac{1}{\frac{0.10}{12} + 1}\right)^{12}} \right]$$

$$\approx \$246.16.$$

To find the total payment A, we simply multiply the monthly payment (rounded to the nearest cent) by the number of payments.

Total Payment = (Number of Payments)(Monthly Payment)

$$A = NM$$

Thus, in Example 1, the total payment for the $2800.00 loan is

$$A = NM = (12)(\$246.16) = \$2953.92. \qquad \blacklozenge$$

Try one!

Robert Burkhardt wants to buy an old car to restore. To do so he borrows $2500.00 that he plans to repay in 18 monthly payments. If the annual percentage rate is $11\frac{1}{2}\%$, what is the monthly payment and what is the total payment?

Monthly Payment:_____   Total Payment: _____

The Truth-In-Lending Law applies to installment loans as well as to time notes. A Truth-In-Lending disclosure form for installment loans is shown in Table 3. Note that the amount and due date of each monthly payment must be specified on the disclosure form.

TABLE 3   DISCLOSURES REQUIRED BY FEDERAL TRUTH-IN-LENDING LAW

Loan proceeds .... $_____   You are required to make _____ equal **Monthly Payments** of $_____

Other charges .... $_____   beginning on _____ 19_____ followed by a **Final Monthly Payment**

Amount financed .... $_____   of $_____.

Finance charge .... $_____

Annual Percentage Rate   *Total Payment*... $_____

_____%

In the event any payment becomes more than 15 days past due, a charge of **$2.50** or **5%** of past due payment, whichever is less, may be charged.

Up to **15%** of the total amount of this note may be charged to cover attorney fees and court costs for collection.

EXAMPLE 2   Finding the monthly payment and the finance charge

In addition to working part time, Denise McDonald borrowed money to help put herself through college. During her freshman, sophomore, junior, and senior years, she borrowed $1000.00, $1500.00, $2000.00, and $2500.00, respectively. Each of these loans was obtained through Denise's home town bank under the Student Loan Guaranty Program. Under the conditions of her loan, Denise pays no interest until nine months after she graduates. At that time she begins to make monthly payments for ten years at the annual percentage rate of 7%. What is Denise's monthly payment and what is the finance charge for this loan?

SOLUTION

To find M, we observe that $P = \$7000.00$, $R = 0.07$, and $N = 120$. Thus,

$$M = P\left[\frac{\frac{R}{12}}{1 - \left(\frac{1}{\frac{R}{12} + 1}\right)^N}\right]$$

$$= (\$7000.00)\left[\frac{\frac{0.07}{12}}{1 - \left(\frac{1}{\frac{0.07}{12} + 1}\right)^{120}}\right]$$

$$\approx \$81.28.$$

The total payment is

$$A = NM = (120)(\$81.28) = \$9753.60$$

and the finance charge is

$$F = A - P = \$9753.60 - \$7000.00 = \$2753.60. \qquad \blacklozenge$$

Try one!

Joni Richardson borrowed money to help put herself through culinary school. She borrowed $1500.00 the first year and $2500.00 the second year. The conditions of this loan stipulate that Joni pay no interest until six months after she graduates. At that time she begins to make monthly payments for five years at the annual percentage rate of 6.5%. What is Joni's monthly payment and what is the finance charge for this loan?

Monthly Payment: _____   Finance Charge: _____

When borrowing money on the installment plan, there are usually several options given as to the term of the loan. For medium-sized loans, you may be given the option to repay the loan in 6, 12, 18, 24, 30, or 36 monthly payments. The greater the number of payments, the less each payment will be. Thus, if your budget is cramped at the time you take out a loan, you may want to opt for many monthly payments. However, you should keep in mind that the longer you keep someone else's money, the greater your finance charge.

As N increases, the monthly payment decreases.
As N increases, the finance charge increases.

To demonstrate this relationship, consider a situation in which $1000.00 is borrowed at an annual percentage rate of 12%. Table 4 shows the monthly payment, the total payment, and the finance charge as the term of the loan varies from six months to 36 months.

TABLE 4 $1000.00 LOAN AT 12% WITH VARYING NUMBER OF PAYMENTS

N, Number of Payments	P, Amount Financed	M, Monthly Payment	A, Total Payment	F, Finance Charge
6	$1000.00	$172.55	$1035.30	$35.30
12	$1000.00	$88.85	$1066.20	$66.20
18	$1000.00	$60.98	$1097.64	$97.64
24	$1000.00	$47.07	$1129.68	$129.68
30	$1000.00	$38.75	$1162.50	$162.50
36	$1000.00	$33.21	$1195.56	$195.56

EXAMPLE 3   Finding the term of a loan given a desired monthly payment

Frank Wilson decides to buy an engagement ring costing $949.00. After making a down payment, he wishes to finance $800.00 and repay the loan in monthly installments. Frank estimates that his budget can accommodate a monthly payment of up to $50.00. If the annual percentage rate is 15%, and he is given the option of 6, 12, 18, 24, or 30 months to repay, what is the shortest term he can choose for the loan that allows him to stay within his budget?

SOLUTION

Since Frank intends to make payments of no more than $50.00 per month, we know that he must make more than 12 payments since

$$(12)(\$50.00) = \$600.00 < \$800.00.$$

For 18 months, the monthly payment is

$$M = P\left[\dfrac{\dfrac{R}{12}}{1 - \left(\dfrac{1}{\dfrac{R}{12} + 1}\right)^N}\right]$$

$$= (\$800.00)\left[\dfrac{\dfrac{0.15}{12}}{1 - \left(\dfrac{1}{\dfrac{0.15}{12} + 1}\right)^{18}}\right]$$

$$\approx \$49.91.$$

Therefore, if Frank chooses to repay his loan in 18 months, his monthly payment of $49.91 will be less than his budgeted $50.00. ◆

Try one!

Lynette Royerson wants to buy a gold ring for her mother's 40th birthday. The ring costs $350.00. Lynette has $35.00 for a down payment and she decides to finance the remaining amount at an annual percentage rate of 13%. If Lynette is given the option of 6, 12, 18, 24, or 30 monthly payments, what is the shortest term she can choose for the loan that allow her to stay with her budget of $35.00 per month?

Answer: _____

As each monthly payment is made on an installment loan, the lending institution divides the payment into two categories. Part of each payment is **payment toward the interest** (or finance charge) and part is **payment toward the principal**. To illustrate this process, consider the loan described in Example 1, in which $2800.00 is borrowed at 10% for a year with monthly payments of $246.16. When the first monthly payment is made, the entire $2800.00 has been kept for one month. One month's interest on this amount is

$$\text{Monthly Interest} = (\text{Balance Before Payment})(\text{Rate})(\text{Time})$$

$$= (\$2800.00)(0.10)\left(\tfrac{1}{12}\right)$$

$$\approx \$23.33.$$

(Note that for installment loans with monthly payments, the time between payments is usually figured as $\frac{1}{12}$ of a year.) Now, since $23.33 of the first monthly payment is for interest, we must deduct $23.33 from the monthly payment to find the amount applied toward the principal. That is

$246.16	monthly payment
− 23.33	interest payment
$222.83	principal payment

and after one month the **balance** of the loan is

$2800.00	balance before payment
− 222.83	principal payment
$2577.17	balance after payment

During the *second month*, the balance is only $2577.17 (not the full $2800.00), so the interest during this period will not be as great. Specifically, the second interest payment is

$$\text{Interest} = (\$2577.17)(0.10)\left(\tfrac{1}{12}\right)$$

$$\approx \$21.48$$

and the second principal payment is

$246.16	monthly payment
− 21.48	interest payment
$224.68	principal payment

The complete record of monthly payments for an installment loan showing the interest payments, the principal payments, and the balances before and after each payment is called an amortization schedule. Table 5 shows an **amortization schedule** for the loan described in Example 1.

TABLE 5	AMORTIZATION SCHEDULE FOR $2800.00 LOAN AT 10% FOR 12 MONTHS				
Payment Number	Balance Before Payment	Payment	Interest Payment	Principal Payment	Balance After Payment
1	$2800.00	$246.16	$23.33	$222.83	$2577.17
2	$2577.17	$246.16	$21.48	$224.68	$2352.49
3	$2352.49	$246.16	$19.60	$226.56	$2125.93
4	$2125.93	$246.16	$17.72	$228.44	$1897.49
5	$1897.49	$246.16	$15.81	$230.35	$1667.14
6	$1667.14	$246.16	$13.89	$232.27	$1434.87
7	$1434.87	$246.16	$11.96	$234.20	$1200.67
8	$1200.67	$246.16	$10.01	$236.15	$964.52
9	$964.52	$246.16	$8.04	$238.12	$726.40
10	$726.40	$246.16	$6.05	$240.11	$486.29
11	$486.29	$246.16	$4.05	$242.11	$244.18
12	$244.18	$246.21	$2.03	$244.18	$0.00

Note that the final payment shown in Table 5 is $246.21 rather than the $246.16. This difference is due to round off error in calculating the monthly payment. To find the final payment in an amortization schedule, we add the balance before the final payment to the final interest payment. Thus, in Table 5 the final payment is

$244.18   balance before final payment
+   2.03   final interest payment
$246.21   final payment.

To avoid the inconvenience of having a final payment that differs from the others, many lending institutions prefer to lend money only in increments for which all of the payments are equal. Example 4 illustrates such a case.

EXAMPLE 4   **Constructing an amortization schedule**

Construct an amortization schedule for a six-month installment loan of $802.35 at an annual percentage rate of 12.75%.

SOLUTION

The monthly payment on this loan is

$$M = P\left[\frac{\frac{R}{12}}{1 - \left(\frac{1}{\frac{R}{12} + 1}\right)^N}\right]$$

$$= (\$802.35)\left[\frac{\frac{0.1275}{12}}{1 - \left(\frac{1}{\frac{0.1275}{12} + 1}\right)^6}\right]$$

$$\approx \$138.74.$$

The following equations are used to complete an amortization schedule:

Interest Payment = (Balance before payment)(Rate)(Time)

Principal Payment = Monthly payment − Interest payment

Balance After Payment = Balance before payment − Principal payment

Final Payment = Interest payment + Balance before payment

The first row of the amortization schedule for this loan may be calculated as follows:

Calculator Steps	Display
802.35 STO	802.35
☒ 0.1275 ÷ 12 =	8.52496875
CE/C 8.52	8.52
+⊂− + 138.74 =	130.22
+⊂− + RCL = STO	672.13
Return to step 2	

The complete amortization schedule is shown in Table 6.

TABLE 6 — AMORTIZATION SCHEDULE FOR $802.35 LOAN AT 12.75% FOR SIX MONTHS

Payment Number	Balance Before Payment	Payment	Interest Payment	Principal Payment	Balance After Payment
1	$802.35	$138.74	$8.52	$130.22	$672.13
2	$672.13	$138.74	$7.14	$131.60	$540.53
3	$540.53	$138.74	$5.74	$133.00	$407.53
4	$407.53	$138.74	$4.33	$134.41	$273.12
5	$273.12	$138.74	$2.90	$135.84	$137.28
6	$137.28	$138.74	$1.46	$137.28	$0.00

Notice from the amortization schedules shown in Tables 5 and 6 that most of the interest on installment loans is paid in the early stages of repayment. ◆

Try one!

Construct an amortization schedule for a six month installment loan of $1000.00 at an annual percentage rate of 9.5%.

Payment Number	Balance Before Payment	Payment	Interest Payment	Principal Payment	Balance After Payment
1					
2					
3					
4					
5					
6					

| EXAMPLE 5 | **Finding the portion of the finance charge paid after K payments** |

The first six rows of an amortization schedule are shown in Table 7. What is the finance charge for this loan and what percentage of the finance charge is paid in the first six payments?

| **T A B L E   7** | AMORTIZATION SCHEDULE FOR $2000.00 LOAN AT 12.5% FOR 18 MONTHS |

Payment Number	Balance Before Payment	Payment	Interest Payment	Principal Payment	Balance After Payment
1	$2000.00	$122.43	$20.83	$101.60	$1898.40
2	$1898.40	$122.43	$19.78	$102.65	$1795.75
3	$1795.75	$122.43	$18.71	$103.72	$1692.03
4	$1692.03	$122.43	$17.63	$104.80	$1587.23
5	$1587.23	$122.43	$16.53	$105.90	$1481.33
6	$1481.33	$122.43	$15.43	$107.00	$1374.33

SOLUTION

The total payment for this loan is

$$A = NM = (18)(\$122.43) = \$2203.74$$

and the finance charge is

$$F = A - P = \$2203.74 - \$2000.00 = \$203.74.$$

Finally, since the interest paid in the first six payments is

$$\$20.83 + \$19.78 + \$18.71 + \$17.63$$

$$+ \$16.53 + \$15.43 = \$108.91,$$

the percentage of the finance charge paid in the first six months of this 18-month installment loan is

$$\frac{\$108.91}{\$203.74} \approx 0.5346 = 53.46\%. \qquad \blacklozenge$$

Try one!

The first six rows of an 18-month amortization schedule are shown below. What is the finance charge for this loan and what percentage of the finance charge is paid in the first six months?

Payment Number	Balance Before Payment	Payment	Interest Payment	Principal Payment	Balance After Payment
1	$2500.00	$153.62	$27.08	$126.54	$2373.46
2	$2373.46	$153.62	$25.71	$127.91	$2245.55
3	$2245.55	$153.62	$24.33	$129.29	$2116.26
4	$2116.26	$153.62	$22.93	$130.69	$1985.57
5	$1985.57	$153.62	$21.51	$132.11	$1853.46
6	$1853.46	$153.62	$20.08	$133.54	$1719.92

Finance Charge: _____

Percentage: _____

After a person has obtained an installment loan, it may happen that he or she wishes to repay the loan earlier than called for in the original term of the loan. To do this, the borrower may contact the lending institution and ask for a "pay-off" figure or the **balance due**. For example, if the loan illustrated in Table 7 were paid off *at the time of the fourth payment*, the balance due would be

$1692.03   balance after third payment

+ 17.63   interest

$1709.66   balance due.

In general, the balance due on an installment loan is given by

Balance Due = Balance after last payment

+ Interest since last payment.

EXAMPLE 6   **Finding the balance due for early payoff of a loan**

Margo Green obtains an installment loan for $10,000.00 to build an extra bedroom onto her home. The loan is taken out for seven years at an annual percentage rate of 11.5%. Sometime after the second payment is made, Margo receives an inheritance that allows her to pay off the loan completely. If Margo's monthly payment is $173.86, and she decides to pay off the loan when the third payment is due, what will the balance be at the time she pays off the loan?

SOLUTION

The first two lines in the amortization schedule for this loan are shown in Table 8.

	TABLE 8	AMORTIZATION SCHEDULE FOR $10,000.00 LOAN AT 11.5% FOR SEVEN YEARS			
Payment Number	Balance Before Payment	Payment	Interest Payment	Principal Payment	Balance After Payment
1	$10,000.00	$173.86	$95.83	$78.03	$9921.97
2	$9921.97	$173.86	$95.09	$78.77	$9843.20

From Table 8 we see that the balance after Margo's second payment is $9843.20. Since Margo wants to pay off the loan one month after the second payment was made, her balance due must include the interest on $9543.20 for one month. Finally, since this interest amounts to

$$\text{Interest} = (\$9843.20)(0.115)\left(\tfrac{1}{12}\right) \approx \$94.33,$$

the balance due is

$9843.20	balance after second payment
+ 94.33	interest for one month
$9937.53	balance due.

◆

Try one!

Below are the first three lines in the amortization schedule for a $1600.00 loan at 15% for 12 months.

Payment Number	Balance Before Payment	Payment	Interest Payment	Principal Payment	Balance After Payment
1	$1600.00	$144.41	$20.00	$124.41	$1475.59
2	$1475.59	$144.41	$18.44	$125.97	$1349.62
3	$1349.62	$144.41	$16.87	$127.54	$122.08

If the borrower decides to pay off the loan when the fourth payment is due, how much will the balance due be at that time?

Answer: _____

We conclude this section with a comment on rounding procedures. In computing monthly payments and amortization schedules, some lending institutions follow the procedure of *rounding to the nearest cent*. Other lending institutions give themselves a slight advantage by always *rounding up to the next highest cent* when calculating interest due to them. In most transactions, the total difference in these two rounding procedures should amount to only a few pennies.

Important Terms

A, total payment

amortization

amortization schedule

balance due

F, finance charge

installments

installment loan

interest payment

M, monthly payment

N, number of monthly payments

P, principal or amount financed

principal payment

R, annual percentage rate

Important Formulas

$$M = P \left[\frac{\frac{R}{12}}{1 - \left(\frac{1}{\frac{R}{12} + 1} \right)^N} \right]$$

$$A = NM$$

$$F = A - P$$

Interest Payment = (Balance before payment)(Rate)(Time)

Principal Payment = Monthly payment − Interest payment

Balance After Payment = Balance before payment − Principal payment

Final Payment = Interest payment + Balance before payment

CONSUMER HINTS

• Arrange to pay off an installment loan with as few payments as you can afford. Remember that as the number of payments increases, the finance charge also increases.

• Do not make a decision to accept an installment loan on the size of monthly payments alone. Be sure to examine a Truth-In-Lending Law declaration indicating the annual percentage rate of your loan *before* you sign any papers.

• Do not decide upon a particular lending source until you have compared its annual percentage rate with those of other sources. Often the least expensive lending source is one with which you already conduct some business, such as your bank or credit union.

SECTION 2   EXERCISES

In Exercises 1–4, find (a) the monthly payment, (b) the total payment, and (c) the finance charge.

1. An installment loan for $1500.00 is to be repaid in 12 monthly payments with an annual percentage rate of 20%.

   Monthly Payment: _____

   Total Payment: _____

   Finance Charge: _____

2. An installment loan for $400.00 is to be repaid in six monthly payments with an annual percentage rate of 18%.

   Monthly Payment: _____

   Total Payment: _____

   Finance Charge: _____

3. An installment loan for $20,000.00 is to be repaid in equal monthly payments for 15 years with an annual percentage rate of 9%.

Monthly Payment: _____

Total Payment: _____

Finance Charge: _____

4. An installment loan for $20,000.00 is to be repaid in equal monthly payments for ten years with an annual percentage rate of 9%.

Monthly Payment: _____

Total Payment: _____

Finance Charge: _____

5. Sally Blackstone takes out a $1000.00 installment loan at an annual percentage rate of 14%. If Sally can afford to make payments of no more than $50.00 per month, which of the following terms should Sally request?

    a. 6 months   **b.** 12 months   **c.** 18 months   **d.** 24 months   **e.** 30 months

Answer: _____

6. Marge and Ken Young take out an installment loan for $2600.00 at an annual percentage rate of 18%. If they can afford to make payments of no more than $100.00 per month, which of the following terms should they request?

    a. 12 months   **b.** 24 months   **c.** 36 months   **d.** 48 months

Answer: _____

7. For the loan in Exercise 5, suppose that Sally could afford payments of up to $65.00 per month. Which term should she now choose and how much would she save in finance charges by choosing this shorter term?

Term: _____   Savings: _____

8. For the loan in Exercise 6, suppose that Marge and Ken could afford payments of up to $130.00 per month. Which term should they now choose and how much would they save in finance charges by choosing this shorter term?

Term: _____   Savings: _____

In Exercises 9–18, consider a $500.00 installment loan to be repaid in six months with an annual percentage rate of $11\frac{1}{2}\%$.

9. Find the monthly payment.

Answer: _____

10. Find the interest payment for the first month.

Answer: _____

11. Find the balance after one payment.

Answer: _____

12. Find the interest payment for the second month.

Answer: _____

13. Continue the process started in Exercises 10-12 to form an amortization schedule covering the entire term of this loan.

Payment Number	Balance Before Payment	Payment	Interest Payment	Principal Payment	Balance After Payment
1	_____	_____	_____	_____	_____
2	_____	_____	_____	_____	_____
3	_____	_____	_____	_____	_____
4	_____	_____	_____	_____	_____
5	_____	_____	_____	_____	_____
6	_____	_____	_____	_____	_____

14. Find the percentage of the total finance charge for this loan paid after the first payment.

Answer: _____

15. Find the percentage of the total finance charge for this loan paid after the first two payments.

Answer: _____

16. Suppose this loan were paid off at the time of the third monthly payment. What would the balance due be at this time?

Answer: _____

17. Suppose this loan were paid off at the time of the fourth monthly payment. What would the balance due be at this time?

Answer: _____

18. How much is saved in finance charges if the loan is paid off at the time of the third monthly payment?

Answer: _____

19. The Austins are buying a sofa by financing $900.00 on an installment plan in which the annual percentage rate is 16%. They have a choice of repaying the loan in 12 monthly installments or 18 monthly installments.

   a. What is the monthly payment for each plan?

   12-month plan: _____

   18-month plan: _____

   b. What is the finance charge for each plan?

   12-month plan: _____

   18-month plan: _____

   c. What is one advantage of each plan?

   12-month plan:_____

   _____

   18-month plan:_____

   _____

20. Vera and Jim Kranz are buying a new freezer that costs $749.95 plus 6% sales tax. They make a $100.00 down payment and pay the remainder on an installment plan at an annual percentage rate of $14\frac{1}{2}\%$. They have the choice of repaying the loan in six monthly installments or in 12 monthly installments.

a. What is the monthly payment for each plan?

6-month plan: _____

12-month plan: _____

b. What is the finance charge for each plan?

6-month plan: _____

12-month plan: _____

c. What is one advantage of each plan?

6-month plan: _____

_____

12-month plan:_____

_____

21. Benjamin Scott buys a lawn and garden tractor and decides to borrow $1200.00 at an annual percentage rate of $10\frac{1}{2}\%$ to be repaid in nine monthly installments. Construct an amortization schedule for this loan.

Payment Number	Balance Before Payment	Payment	Interest Payment	Principal Payment	Balance After Payment
1	_____	_____	_____	_____	_____
2	_____	_____	_____	_____	_____
3	_____	_____	_____	_____	_____
4	_____	_____	_____	_____	_____
5	_____	_____	_____	_____	_____
6	_____	_____	_____	_____	_____
7	_____	_____	_____	_____	_____
8	_____	_____	_____	_____	_____
9	_____	_____	_____	_____	_____

22. Construct an amortization schedule for a $750.00 installment loan at 14% annual percentage rate taken out over nine months.

Payment Number	Balance Before Payment	Payment	Interest Payment	Principal Payment	Balance After Payment
1	_____	_____	_____	_____	_____
2	_____	_____	_____	_____	_____
3	_____	_____	_____	_____	_____
4	_____	_____	_____	_____	_____
5	_____	_____	_____	_____	_____
6	_____	_____	_____	_____	_____
7	_____	_____	_____	_____	_____
8	_____	_____	_____	_____	_____
9	_____	_____	_____	_____	_____

23. Arlene Thompson borrows $2000.00 to purchase a piano. She has a choice of obtaining the loan from two different sources. One source offers her the loan for 24 monthly payments at an annual percentage rate of 14%. The second source offers the loan for 18 monthly payments at an annual percentage rate of 16%. Assuming that she can afford the monthly payments for either plan, which should she choose in order to minimize her finance charges?

Answer: _____

Section 3

Financing a New Car

Most people put a great deal of thought into the purchase of a new car. Decisions must be made concerning the make of the car, the performance, size, color, and options that best suit their needs, wants and resources. With the availability of various consumer publications, a prospective buyer can compare the cost, performance, gas mileage, and repair records of literally dozens of different types of cars. Surprisingly, after putting much time and energy into shopping for the right car, many consumers spend very little time shopping for the most economical means of financing their new purchase.

Millions of automobiles are sold in the United States every year, and by far most of these are financed with monthly payments, usually from two to five years. It is difficult to find a new car today that costs less than $10,000.00, and painfully easy to find new car prices running higher than $20,000.00. With so much money involved in buying a car, it makes good sense to put careful thought, not only into the make and model of the car you buy, but also into the method of financing your new purchase.

Generally, advertisements for new cars list the **base price** of various car models; however, this base price usually bears little resemblance to the total cost of a car. Example 1 describes a typical situation.

EXAMPLE 1   Finding the total cost of a new car

Bill Engel buys a new automobile whose base price is $15,000.00. In addition to the base price, Bill orders $950.00 worth of options for the car. Bill must also pay a destination charge of $507.00, a sales tax of $987.42, a closing cost of $40.00, and a licensing and registration fee of $49.00. After making a down payment of $2533.42, Bill finances the remaining cost at an annual percentage rate of 8% for 60 monthly payments (five years). What is the total cost of Bill's car including the finance charge?

55

SOLUTION

To find the amount financed, we proceed as follows:

$15,000.00	base price
950.00	price of options
507.00	destination charge
435.96	sales tax
40.00	closing cost
+ 49.00	license and registration fee
$17,533.42	total
− 2533.42	down payment
$15,000.00	amount financed.

The monthly payment on this amount for five years with $R = 0.08$ is

$$M = P\left[\frac{\frac{R}{12}}{1 - \left(\frac{1}{\frac{R}{12} + 1}\right)^N}\right]$$

$$= (\$15,000.00)\left[\frac{\frac{0.08}{12}}{1 - \left(\frac{1}{\frac{0.08}{12} + 1}\right)^{60}}\right]$$

$$\approx \$304.15.$$

Thus, Bill's total payment for the loan is

$$A = NM = 60(\$304.15) = \$18,249.00.$$

Finally, including Bill's initial down payment, the total cost of the car is

$18,249.00	total loan payment
+ 2533.42	down payment
$20,782.42	total cost of car.

◆

Try one!

Jim Stone buys a new automobile whose base price is $14,500.00. In addition to the base price, Jim orders $675.00 worth of options for the car. Jim must also pay a destination charge of $495.00, a sales tax of $940.20, a closing cost of $40.00, and a licensing and registration fee of $50.00. After making a down payment of $2200.20, Jim finances the remaining cost at an annual percentage rate of 7% for 60 monthly payments. What is the total cost of Jim's car including the finance charge?

Answer: _____

When purchasing a new car, you should be aware of a variety of charges and credits. The **base price** of a car is the price of the car without any **options**. What is or is not considered optional varies with the model, but typical options are automatic transmission, antilock brakes, security system, stereo, tinted glass, air conditioning, and cruise control. The **destination charge** is the cost of shipping the car from the manufacturer to the dealer. The **list price** (or sticker price) is the sum of the base price, the price of options, and the destination charge. **Credit toward trade-in** is the price the dealer is willing to give for the buyer's present car, less any money the buyer may still owe on that car. The **taxable amount of the sale** depends on the state in which the car is being purchased. In some states, sales tax is computed on the list price. In other states, the credit toward trade-in is subtracted from this sum before the sales tax is computed. The **closing cost** is the sum of any legal or notary fees connected with the sale of the car. Finally, to license and register the car, there is a state **licensing and registration fee**. Table 9 shows an example of a car sales record.

TABLE 9   ITEMIZED RECORD OF AUTOMOBILE SALE

Base Price	$12,489.00	List Price	$17,094.00
Options		*Credit for trade-in*	− 5,000.00
Keyless remote entry system	190.00	Taxable Amount of Sale*	$12,094.00
Leather Interior	490.00	*Sales tax*	725.64
Air conditioning	795.00	*Closing cost*	40.00
Antilock brakes	570.00	*Registration*	+ 48.00
Rear window defroster	190.00	Total	$12,907.64
Sun roof	595.00	*Down payment*	− 1907.64
Power Windows	340.00	Amount Financed	$11,000.00
Cruise control	215.00		
AM/FM stereo and CD player	455.00		
Power seats	+ 290.00		
Subtotal	$16,619.00		
Destination charge	+ 475.00		
List Price	$17,094.00		

*In some states, the taxable amount would be $17,094.00

The buyer of the car whose sale is illustrated in Table 9 needs to finance $11,000.00. The monthly payments for such a loan could vary from $502.53 ($R = 0.09$, $N = 24$) to $202.58 ($R = 0.04$, $N = 60$). To help you see how monthly payments can vary we list in Table 10 the monthly payments corresponding to several different terms, annual percentage rates, and amounts.

TABLE 10 MONTHLY PAYMENTS FOR VARIOUS TERMS, RATES, AND AMOUNTS

Annual Percentage Rate	Amount Financed	Number of Months						
		24	30	36	42	48	54	60
4%	$12,000.00	$521.10	$421.00	$354.29	$306.66	$270.95	$243.19	$221.00
	$13,000.00	$564.52	$456.08	$383.81	$332.21	$293.53	$263.46	$239.41
	$14,000.00	$607.95	$491.17	$413.34	$357.77	$316.11	$283.72	$257.83
	$15,000.00	$651.37	$526.25	$442.86	$383.32	$338.69	$303.99	$276.25
	$16,000.00	$694.80	$561.33	$472.38	$408.87	$361.26	$324.25	$294.66
	$17,000.00	$738.22	$596.42	$501.91	$434.43	$383.84	$344.52	$313.08
	$18,000.00	$781.65	$631.50	$531.43	$459.98	$406.42	$364.79	$331.50
5%	$12,000.00	$526.46	$426.35	$359.65	$312.04	$276.35	$248.62	$226.45
	$13,000.00	$570.33	$461.88	$389.62	$338.04	$299.38	$269.34	$245.33
	$14,000.00	$614.20	$497.41	$419.59	$364.04	$322.41	$290.06	$264.20
	$15,000.00	$658.07	$532.94	$449.56	$390.05	$345.44	$310.77	$283.07
	$16,000.00	$701.94	$568.47	$479.53	$416.05	$368.47	$331.49	$301.94
	$17,000.00	$745.81	$604.00	$509.51	$442.05	$391.50	$352.21	$320.81
	$18,000.00	$789.69	$639.53	$539.48	$468.05	$414.53	$372.93	$339.68
6%	$12,000.00	$531.85	$431.75	$365.06	$317.47	$281.82	$254.12	$231.99
	$13,000.00	$576.17	$467.73	$395.49	$343.93	$305.31	$275.30	$251.33
	$14,000.00	$620.49	$503.70	$425.91	$370.39	$328.79	$296.48	$270.66
	$15,000.00	$664.81	$539.68	$456.33	$396.84	$352.28	$317.65	$289.99
	$16,000.00	$709.13	$575.66	$486.75	$423.30	$375.76	$338.83	$309.32
	$17,000.00	$753.45	$611.64	$517.17	$449.76	$399.25	$360.01	$328.66
	$18,000.00	$797.77	$647.62	$547.59	$476.21	$422.73	$381.18	$347.99
7%	$12,000.00	$537.27	$437.18	$370.53	$322.97	$287.35	$259.70	$237.61
	$13,000.00	$582.04	$473.61	$401.40	$349.88	$311.30	$281.34	$257.42
	$14,000.00	$626.82	$510.05	$432.28	$376.80	$335.25	$302.98	$277.22
	$15,000.00	$671.59	$546.48	$463.16	$403.71	$359.19	$324.62	$297.02
	$16,000.00	$716.36	$582.91	$494.03	$430.63	$383.14	$346.27	$316.82
	$17,000.00	$761.13	$619.34	$524.91	$457.54	$407.09	$367.91	$336.62
	$18,000.00	$805.91	$655.77	$555.79	$484.46	$431.03	$389.55	$356.42
8%	$12,000.00	$542.73	$442.66	$376.04	$328.52	$292.96	$265.35	$243.32
	$13,000.00	$587.95	$479.55	$407.37	$355.90	$317.37	$287.46	$263.59
	$14,000.00	$633.18	$516.44	$438.71	$383.28	$341.78	$309.57	$283.87
	$15,000.00	$678.41	$553.32	$470.05	$410.65	$366.19	$331.69	$304.15
	$16,000.00	$723.64	$590.21	$501.38	$438.03	$390.61	$353.80	$324.42
	$17,000.00	$768.86	$627.10	$532.72	$465.41	$415.02	$375.91	$344.70
	$18,000.00	$814.09	$663.99	$564.05	$492.79	$439.43	$398.02	$364.98
9%	$12,000.00	$548.22	$448.18	$381.60	$334.13	$298.62	$271.07	$249.10
	$13,000.00	$593.90	$485.53	$413.40	$361.98	$323.51	$293.66	$269.86
	$14,000.00	$639.59	$522.87	$445.20	$389.82	$348.39	$316.25	$290.62
	$15,000.00	$685.27	$560.22	$477.00	$417.67	$373.28	$338.84	$311.38
	$16,000.00	$730.96	$597.57	$508.80	$445.51	$398.16	$361.43	$332.13
	$17,000.00	$776.64	$634.92	$540.60	$473.36	$423.05	$384.02	$352.89
	$18,000.00	$822.33	$672.27	$572.40	$501.20	$447.93	$406.61	$373.65

EXAMPLE 2 Fitting the amount financed to a budgeted monthly payment

Ruth Pisani plans to buy a new car. She calls her bank and determines that the "blue-book" trade-in value she can expect for her current car is around $4000.00. In addition to this amount, she has saved $1000.00 to use as a down payment. Ruth wants her monthly payments to be under $300.00 for a term of four years. At an annual percentage rate of 5%, how much can she afford to have financed, and what range of automobile list prices can she afford? (Assume that there is a 6% sales tax calculated on the list price of the new car after the credit for trade in is applied.)

SOLUTION

From Table 10, we can see that a loan of $13,000.00 for 48 months at 5% corresponds to a monthly payment of $299.38. Thus, Ruth should plan on financing $13,000.00 or less. This means she has approximately $18,000.00 to spend on a car:

$4,000.00	credit toward trade-in
1,000.00	down payment
+ 13,000.00	amount financed
$18,000.00	

Figuring destination charges, sales tax, and registration fees to run between $1300.00 and $1500.00, she should be hunting for a list price between $16,500.00 and $16,700.00. ◆

Try one!

Joe Learn plans to buy a new car. The trade-in value for his car is around $3500.00. In addition to this amount, he has saved $2000.00 to use as a down payment. Joe wants his monthly payment to be less than $400.00 for three years. At an annual percentage rate of 6%, how much can he afford to have financed?

Answer: _____

EXAMPLE 3   **Comparing the total cost for small and large down payments**

Janice and George Olson are buying a new car with the following breakdown of costs:

$13,570.00	base price
925.00	price of options
+ 480.00	destination charge
$14,975.00	taxable amount*
+ 748.75	sales tax
$15,723.75	
− 3200.00	trade-in
$12,523.75	
45.00	closing cost
+ 50.00	license and registration fee
$12,618.75.	

They are asked to put a least $1000.00 down and are told they can finance the rest at 6% (annual percentage rate) for five years. Janice and George have a total of $3500.00 they could use as a down payment. By making this larger down payment, they figure that they can handle monthly payments for three years instead of five. What is the total cost of the car (including finance charges) if

a. they put $1000.00 down and make 60 payments?

b. they put $3500.00 down and make 36 payments?

SOLUTION

a. For a down payment of $1000.00, the amount financed is $11,618.75 and the monthly payment for 60 months is

$$M = P\left[\frac{\frac{R}{12}}{1 - \left(\frac{1}{\frac{R}{12} + 1}\right)^N}\right]$$

$$= (\$11,618.75)\left[\frac{\frac{0.06}{12}}{1 - \left(\frac{1}{\frac{0.06}{12} + 1}\right)^{60}}\right]$$

$$\approx \$224.62.$$

*The Olsons live in a state where the sales tax is calculated before subtracting the trade-in credit.

Thus, their total payment is $A = 60(\$224.62) = \$13{,}477.20$ and the total cost of the car is

$13,477.20	total payment on loan
1,000.00	down payment
+ 3,200.00	trade-in
$17,677.20	total cost of car

b. For a down payment of $3500.00, the amount financed is $9118.75 and the monthly payment for 36 months is

$$M = P\left[\dfrac{\frac{R}{12}}{1 - \left(\dfrac{1}{\frac{R}{12} + 1}\right)^{N}}\right]$$

$$= (\$9118.75)\left[\dfrac{\frac{0.06}{12}}{1 - \left(\dfrac{1}{\frac{0.06}{12} + 1}\right)^{36}}\right]$$

$$\approx \$277.41.$$

Now, the total loan payment is $A = 36(\$277.41) = \$9986.76$ and the total cost of the car is

$9986.76	total payment on loan
3500.00	down payment
+ 3200.00	trade-in
$16,686.76	total cost of car	◆

Try one!

Suppose the Olsons (see Example 3) decide to put $2000.00 down and make 48 payments. What is the total cost of the car including the finance charges?

Answer: _____

One of the discouraging things to car buyers is that cars tend to depreciate almost as rapidly as they are paid off. This is especially true during the first and second years after the purchase of a new car. The trade-in value of a car may drop to 70% of the original value after one year and to as low as 50% after two years. This means that for a car financed over five years with a minimal down payment, the trade-in value of the car after two years may not even cover the balance due on the loan. (See Example 4.)

In Section 2, we looked at a method for calculating the balance due on an installment loan by means of an amortization schedule. For long-term loans, this method is quite tedious. Fortunately, there is a straight-forward formula available for finding the balance due. Specifically, for a monthly installment loan, the balance due after n payments is

$$B = \left(1 + \frac{R}{12}\right)^n \left(P - \frac{12M}{R}\right) + \frac{12M}{R}$$

where R is the annual percentage rate, P is the amount financed, and M is the monthly payment.

Calculator Hints

$$B = \left(1 + \frac{R}{12}\right)^n \left(P - \frac{12M}{R}\right) + \frac{12M}{R}$$

To find the balance due on an installment loan using your calculator, apply the following steps:

1. Divide R by 12 and add 1.

2. Raise to the nth power and store in memory.

3. Multiply M by 12 and divide by R. Write down this result for use in step 6.

4. Change signs and add P.

5. Multiply by memory.

6. Add the result of step 3.

7. Round to the nearest hundredth.

EXAMPLE 4   Finding the balance due

Art Winthrop took out a five-year auto loan for $12,000.00 at 9% (annual percentage rate) with monthly payments of $249.10. After two years, he decides to get another car and wants to use his current car as a trade-in. The car dealer offers Art a trade-in value of $7500.00. Is this enough to pay off Art's loan on his present car?

SOLUTION

To find the balance due on Art's loan, we let $P = \$12,000.00$, $R = 0.09$, $M = \$249.10$, and $n = 24$. The balance due after 24 payments is

$$B = \left(1 + \frac{R}{12}\right)^n \left(P - \frac{12M}{R}\right) + \frac{12M}{R}$$

$$= \left(1 + \frac{0.09}{12}\right)^{24} \left(\$12,000.00 - \frac{12(\$249.10)}{0.09}\right) + \frac{12(\$249.10)}{0.09}$$

$$\approx \$7833.41.$$

EXAMPLE 4

Steps	Display
0.09 ÷ 12 =	0.0075
+ 1 =	1.0075
y^x 24 = STO	1.196413529
12 × 249.10 =	2989.2
÷ 0.09 =	33213.33333
+⁄− + 12,000 =	-21213.33333
× RCL =	-25379.919
+ 33213.33333 =	7833.414327

Thus, the balance due on the loan is $7833.41, and the trade-in allowance of $7500.00 is not enough to pay off the loan. ◆

Try one!

Tammy McCoy took out a five-year auto loan for $15,000.00 at 5% (annual percentage rate) with monthly payments of $283.07. After three years she decides to get another car and wants to use her current car as a trade-in. The car dealer offers Tammy a trade-in value of $6400.00. Is this enough to pay off Tammy's loan on her present car?

Answer: _____

| EXAMPLE 5 | **Finding the finance charge paid in _N_ payments** |

If Bill Engel (see Example 1) made the first payment on his $15,000.00 loan on February 10, 1994, how much interest did he pay on the loan during 1994?

SOLUTION

Since Bill paid 11 payments in 1994, his balance due at the end of 1994 is

$$B = \left(1 + \frac{R}{12}\right)^n \left(P - \frac{12M}{R}\right) + \frac{12M}{R}$$

$$= \left(1 + \frac{0.08}{12}\right)^{11} \left(\$15,000.00 - \frac{12(\$304.15)}{0.08}\right) + \frac{12(\$304.15)}{0.08}$$

$$\approx \$12,677.98.$$

This means that during the first 11 payments, Bill reduced the balance from $15,000.00 to $12,677.98 and the amount paid toward the principal during this time was

$15,000.00	amount financed
−12,677.98	balance after 11 payments
$2,322.02	paid toward principal

Since Bill paid a total of 11($304.15) = $3345.65 during the first 11 payments, the interest paid during this time must have been

$3345.65	total of 11 payments
−2322.02	principal payment
$1023.63	interest payment

Thus, Bill paid $1023.63 in interest on this loan in 1994. ◆

Important Terms

A, total loan payment

list price

B, balance due after *n* payments

M, monthly payment

base price

N, number of monthly payments

closing cost

options

destination charge

P, amount financed

down payment

R, annual percentage rate

F, finance charge

trade-in

license and registration fee

Important Formulas

$$B = \left(1 + \frac{R}{12}\right)^{n}\left(P - \frac{12M}{R}\right) + \frac{12M}{R}$$

CONSUMER HINTS

When you purchase a car, consider the following:

• Make as large a down payment as you can afford. The larger the down payment you can make on a car, the more you will save in finance charges.

• Avoid consumer finance companies for auto loans. You can almost always get a lower annual percentage rate at a bank or credit union.

• Before financing your car through a car dealer, check to see if you can get a lower rate by going *directly* to a bank or credit union.

• Take out your auto loan for as few years as you can afford. By making fewer monthly payments, you will have to pay more per month, but you will save in the long run.

SECTION 3   EXERCISES

1. The manufacturer's suggested base price of a car is $11,497.00. Additional charges include: antilock brakes, $162.00; cruise control, $200.00; destination charge, $350.00. The buyer of this particular car is given a trade-in allowance of $2500.00 after which a sales tax of 6% is computed. If the buyer makes a down payment of $1000.00, what is the amount financed?

Answer: _____

2. The manufacturer's suggested base price of a car is $9868.00. Additional charges include: power windows, $338.00; power steering, $139.00; antilock brakes, $162.00; destination charge, $425.00. A sales tax of 5% is computed on the entire list price. If the buyer of this car makes a down payment of $1000.00, what is the amount financed?

Answer: _____

In Exercises 3–6, find the monthly payment and the finance charge on the purchase of a car if the amount financed is $15,000.00.

3. Term: 36 months, annual percentage rate: 6%.

Monthly Payment: _____   Finance Charge: _____

4. Term: 60 months, annual percentage rate: 4%.

Monthly Payment: _____   Finance Charge: _____

5. Term: 48 months, annual percentage rate: 7%.

Monthly Payment: _____   Finance Charge: _____

6. Term: 54 months, annual percentage rate: 9%.

Monthly Payment: _____   Finance Charge: _____

7. Use Table 10 to find the amount that can be financed at an annual percentage rate of 7% assuming that the borrower wishes to pay no more than $350.00 per month for 48 months.

Answer: _____

8. Use Table 10 to find the amount that can be financed at an annual percentage rate of 5% assuming that the borrower wishes to pay approximately $250.00 per month for 54 months.

Answer: _____

9. After a trade-in allowance, Doris Green must pay $10,495.00 for her new car. Determine her finance charge if the annual percentage rate is 8% and

a. she makes a $1200.00 down payment and finances the remainder over 48 months.

Answer: _____

b. she makes a $3000.00 down payment and finances the remainder over 36 months.

Answer: _____

10. After a trade-in allowance, Tom Harris owes $13,500.00 on his new car. Determine his finance charge if the annual percentage rate is 7% and

    a. he makes a $1500.00 down payment and finances the remainder over 48 months.

Answer: _____

    b. he makes a $3500.00 down payment and finances the remainder over 42 months.

Answer: _____

11. Find the balance due after 12 payments on a 36-month auto loan for $12,000.00 for which the annual percentage rate is 4% and the monthly payment is $354.29.

Answer: _____

12. Find the balance due after 24 payments on a 48-month auto loan for $13,000.00 for which the annual percentage rate is 5% and the monthly payment is $299.38.

Answer: _____

13. For the auto loan described in Exercise 3, complete the following table where n represents the number of payments.

n	Balance due after n payments	Total of first n payments	Principal paid after n payments	Interest paid after n payments
6	$12,683.23	$2737.98	$2316.77	$421.21
12	_____	_____	_____	_____
18	_____	_____	_____	_____
24	_____	_____	_____	_____
30	_____	_____	_____	_____
36	_____	_____	_____	_____

14. Bradley Jacobs purchased a car by financing $13,700.00 for 60 months at an annual percentage rate of 8%. After making the 15th payment, Bradley decided to get a new car. How much must he be given as a trade-in allowance in order to pay off the balance on his loan?

Answer: _____

15. Pat and John Sumners decide to purchase a new car by financing $8000.00 at an annual percentage rate of 9%. If Pat accepts the offer of a part-time job, they will be able to pay off the loan in two years. Without this extra income, they figure they must stretch the payments over four years. The amount they save in finance charges is a factor in making the decision. Determine that amount.

Answer: _____

16. Sharon Conrad purchases a new car by financing $9200.00 at 7% for 48 months. After making 17 payments, Sharon receives an inheritance that allows her to pay off her loan. What was her balance due?

Answer: _____

Section 4

Home Mortgages

Owning a house is part of the great American dream. Buying a house is becoming the great American nightmare. The costs connected with buying (and maintaining) a house have risen so drastically in recent years that they have become prohibitive for many people, especially to those who are thinking of buying their first house. Few people pay cash for a house nowadays. Those who buy (as opposed to rent) usually purchase their houses by making a down payment and financing the remainder through a **home mortgage**.

In a typical home mortgage, there are six parties involved: the builder or previous owner, the real estate agent who is conducting the sale, the new buyer, the lending institution, the government (state, city, and/or county), and various people connected with the **closing costs** (appraisals, attorneys, inspectors, and notaries). The costs involved in a typical home mortgage are listed below.

	amount received by previous owner
+	*realtor's commission*
	list price of home
+	*closing costs*
	total cost of home without financing
−	*down payment*
	amount financed

The amount financed for a house is usually paid by means of mortgaging the house through an installment loan with equal monthly payments over a **term** of 20 to 35 years. Except for the long term involved, the basic features of this type of loan were discussed in Section 2.

The difference between home mortgages and other installment loans is that the long term involved in a typical home mortgage produces a staggering amount of interest paid over the term of the mortgage. This can be seen in Table 11, which compares monthly payments with total payments for home mortgages of various terms, rates, and amounts.

TABLE 11   MONTHLY PAYMENT AND TOTAL PAYMENT FOR VARIOUS TERMS, RATES, AND AMOUNTS

Annual Percentage Rate	Amount Financed	Number of Years							
		20		*25*		*30*		*35*	
		Monthly payment	Total payment	Monthly payment	Total payment	Monthly payment	Total payment	Monthly payment	Total payment
6%	$60,000.00	$429.86	$103,166.40	$386.58	$115,974.00	$359.73	$129,502.80	$342.11	$143,686.20
	$70,000.00	$501.50	$120,360.00	$451.01	$135,303.00	$419.69	$151,088.40	$399.13	$167,634.60
	$80,000.00	$573.14	$137,553.60	$515.44	$154,632.00	$479.64	$172,670.40	$456.15	$191,583.00
	$90,000.00	$644.79	$154,749.60	$579.87	$173,961.00	$539.60	$194,256.00	$513.17	$215,531.40
	$100,000.00	$716.43	$171,943.20	$644.30	$193,290.00	$599.55	$215,838.00	$570.19	$239,479.80
7%	$60,000.00	$465.18	$111,643.20	$424.07	$127,221.00	$399.18	$143,704.80	$383.31	$160,990.20
	$70,000.00	$542.71	$130,250.40	$494.75	$148,425.00	$465.71	$167,655.60	$447.20	$187,824.00
	$80,000.00	$620.24	$148,857.60	$565.42	$169,626.00	$532.24	$191,606.40	$511.09	$214,657.80
	$90,000.00	$697.77	$167,464.80	$636.10	$190,830.00	$598.77	$215,557.20	$574.97	$241,487.40
	$100,000.00	$775.30	$186,072.00	$706.78	$212,034.00	$665.30	$239,508.00	$638.86	$268,321.20
8%	$60,000.00	$501.86	$120,446.40	$463.09	$138,927.00	$440.26	$158,493.60	$426.16	$178,987.20
	$70,000.00	$585.51	$140,522.40	$540.27	$162,081.00	$513.64	$184,910.40	$497.18	$208,815.60
	$80,000.00	$669.15	$160,596.00	$617.45	$185,235.00	$587.01	$211,323.60	$568.21	$238,648.20
	$90,000.00	$752.80	$180,672.00	$694.63	$208,389.00	$660.39	$237,740.40	$639.23	$268,476.60
	$100,000.00	$836.44	$200,745.60	$771.82	$231,546.00	$733.76	$264,153.60	$710.26	$298,309.20
9%	$60,000.00	$539.84	$129,561.60	$503.52	$151,056.00	$482.77	$173,797.20	$470.40	$197,568.00
	$70,000.00	$629.81	$151,154.40	$587.44	$176,232.00	$563.24	$202,766.40	$548.80	$230,496.00
	$80,000.00	$719.78	$172,747.20	$671.36	$201,408.00	$643.70	$231,732.00	$627.19	$263,419.80
	$90,000.00	$809.75	$194,340.00	$755.28	$226,584.00	$724.16	$260,697.60	$705.59	$296,347.80
	$100,000.00	$899.73	$215,935.20	$839.20	$251,760.00	$804.62	$289,663.20	$783.99	$329,275.80
10%	$60,000.00	$579.01	$138,962.40	$545.22	$163,566.00	$526.54	$189,554.40	$515.80	$216,636.00
	$70,000.00	$675.52	$162,124.80	$636.09	$190,827.00	$614.30	$221,148.00	$601.77	$252,743.40
	$80,000.00	$772.02	$185,284.80	$726.96	$218,088.00	$702.06	$252,741.60	$687.74	$288,850.80
	$90,000.00	$868.52	$208,444.80	$817.83	$245,349.00	$789.81	$284,331.60	$773.71	$324,958.20
	$100,000.00	$965.02	$231,604.80	$908.70	$272,610.00	$877.57	$315,925.20	$859.67	$361,061.40
11%	$60,000.00	$619.31	$148,634.40	$588.07	$176,421.00	$571.39	$205,700.40	$562.17	$236,111.40
	$70,000.00	$722.53	$173,407.20	$686.08	$205,824.00	$666.63	$239,986.80	$655.87	$275,465.40
	$80,000.00	$825.75	$198,180.00	$784.09	$235,227.00	$761.86	$274,269.60	$749.57	$314,819.40
	$90,000.00	$928.97	$222,952.80	$882.10	$264,630.00	$857.09	$308,552.40	$843.26	$354,169.20
	$100,000.00	$1032.19	$247,725.60	$980.11	$294,033.00	$952.32	$342,835.20	$936.96	$393,523.20
12%	$60,000.00	$660.65	$158,556.00	$631.93	$189,579.00	$617.17	$222,181.20	$609.33	$255,918.60
	$70,000.00	$770.76	$184,982.40	$737.26	$221,178.00	$720.03	$259,210.80	$710.88	$298,569.60
	$80,000.00	$880.87	$211,408.80	$842.58	$252,774.00	$822.89	$296,240.40	$812.44	$341,224.80
	$90,000.00	$990.98	$237,835.20	$947.90	$284,370.00	$925.75	$333,270.00	$913.99	$383,875.80
	$100,000.00	$1101.09	$264,261.60	$1053.22	$315,966.00	$1028.61	$370,299.60	$1015.55	$426,531.00

EXAMPLE 1   Finding the finance charge using a table

Ellen and Don West are buying a new house. They are financing $80,000.00 at 9% (annual percentage rate). How much will they have to pay in finance charges if they take out a home mortgage for **a.** 20 years? **b.** 35 years?

SOLUTION

a. From Table 11, we see that the monthly payment for 20 years on a $80,000.00 mortgage at 9% is $719.78. Since 20 years corresponds to 240 months, the total payment is

$$A = NM = 240(\$719.78) = \$172,747.20$$

and the finance charge is

$$F = A - P = \$172,747.20 - \$80,000.00 = \$92,747.20.$$

b. For 35 years, the monthly payment is $627.19. In this case, we have $N = 12(35) = 420$, and the total payment is

$$A = NM = 420(\$627.19) = \$263,419.80.$$

Therefore, the finance charge is

$$F = A - P = \$263,419.80 - \$80,000.00 = \$183,419.80. \quad \blacklozenge$$

Try one!

Jeanne and Phillip Langer are buying a new house. They are financing $70,000.00 at 8% (annual percentage rate). How much will they have to pay in finance charges if they take out a home mortgage for 30 years?

Answer: _____

If you are planning to buy a house, you would do well to be familiar with the basic features of home mortgages. Differences in the amount financed, rate, and term can result in huge differences in finance charges. For instance, in Example 1, an increase in the term of the mortgage from 20 to 35 years resulted in an increase in the finance charge from $92,747.20 to $183,419.80. Of course, there is a big difference between 20 years and 35 years, but even slight changes in home mortgages can produce substantial differences in finance charges. For example, in Table 11, we see that an increase of one or two percent in the annual percentage rate can result in an increase in finance charges of several thousand dollars.

Prospective house buyers are often very concerned with the amount of their monthly payment. In an effort to produce smaller monthly payments, they are willing to take out loans over very long terms. However, by studying Table 11 closely, we can see that the monthly payments do not decrease linearly as the term increases. For example, by adding five years to the term of a $60,000.00 mortgage at 11% for 20 years, we can lower the monthly payment from $619.31 to $588.07 (a drop of $31.24). By adding five more years to the term of the mortgage, we only lower the monthly payment from $588.07 to $571.39 (a drop of $16.68). Finally, by adding yet another five years to the term, we only lower the monthly payment from $571.39 to $562.17 (a drop of $9.22).

A good rule to remember when deciding upon the term of a conventional home mortgage is that there is a minimum monthly payment which must be made no matter how many years are in the term of the mortgage. Specifically, if you obtain a mortgage for P dollars at an annual percentage rate of R, then you must make a monthly payment of at least

$$I = PRT = \frac{PR}{12},$$

which is the amount required to cover the interest for keeping P dollars for one month.

EXAMPLE 2   Comparing the monthly payment with the minimum payment

Brenda Warren is buying a home. The costs connected with her purchase are

$80,000.00	list price of home
700.00	title search
50.00	credit report fee
225.00	document preparation
35.00	mortgage recording fee
1,200.00	reimbursement and escrow for taxes
800.00	1% origination fee
800.00	1% transfer tax
90.00	tax service fee
+ 70.00	title endorsement
$83,970.00	
− 8,000.00	10% down payment
$75,970.00	amount financed

If Brenda can obtain a mortgage for 8.5%, what is the minimum monthly payment she must make? What would her monthly payment be for **a.** a 20-year term? **b.** a 30-year term?

SOLUTION

Since Brenda must make payments which (at least) cover the interest on $75,970.00 for one month, the minimum monthly payment would be

$$I = \frac{PR}{12} = \frac{(\$75{,}970.00)(0.085)}{12} \approx \$538.12.$$

a. For a 20-year term, the monthly payment would be

$$M = P\left[\frac{\frac{R}{12}}{1 - \left(\frac{1}{\frac{R}{12} + 1}\right)^N}\right]$$

$$= (\$75{,}970.00)\left[\frac{\frac{0.085}{12}}{1 - \left(\frac{1}{\frac{0.085}{12} + 1}\right)^{240}}\right]$$

$$\approx \$659.29.$$

b. For a 30-year term, the monthly payment would be

$$M = P\left[\frac{\frac{R}{12}}{1 - \left(\frac{1}{\frac{R}{12} + 1}\right)^N}\right]$$

$$= (\$75,970.00)\left[\frac{\frac{0.085}{12}}{1 - \left(\frac{1}{\frac{0.085}{12} + 1}\right)^{360}}\right]$$

$$\approx \$584.14.$$

Try one!

If Brenda Warren (from Example 2) could obtain a mortgage for 9%, what would be the minimum monthly payment? What would be her monthly payment for a 25-year term?

Minimum Payment: _____   Monthly Payment: _____

Note from Example 2 that as the term of the mortgage increases, the actual monthly payment approaches the minimum monthly payment. This principle is demonstrated in Figure 2.

Figure 2

In Section 2 we discussed the amortization of installment loans and noted that the lion's share of the finance charge is paid in the early stages of amortization. For long-term loans (such as home mortgages) this feature of installment loans reaches dramatic proportions, so much so that well over 90% of the early payments in a home mortgage go toward interest. Example 3 describes a typical situation.

EXAMPLE 3   **Comparing the interest payment with the principal payment**

Ruth and Stewart Segal take out a home mortgage of $85,000.00 on a new house at 8.75% for 35 years. The monthly payment is $650.56. Construct an amortization schedule for their first year's payments. How much do they pay in the first year? What percentage of this amount goes toward interest? What percentage goes toward principal?

SOLUTION

The amount toward interest (for the first payment) is given by

$$I = PRT = (\$85,000.00)(0.0875)\left(\tfrac{1}{12}\right) \approx \$619.79.$$

Since the payment is $650.56, the amount toward principal (for the first month) is given by

$650.56	monthly payment
-619.79	interest payment
$30.77	principal payment

Thus, the balance after the first payment is

$85,000.00	balance before first payment
$-$ 30.77	principal payment
$84,969.23	balance after first payment

Continuing this process for 12 payments gives us the schedule shown in Table 12.

T A B L E 12	**AMORTIZATION SCHEDULE FOR $85,000.00 MORTGAGE AT 8.75% FOR 35 YEARS**

Payment Number	Balance Before Payment	Payment	Interest Payment	Principal Payment	Balance After Payment
1	$85,000.00	$650.56	$619.79	$30.77	$84,969.23
2	$84,969.23	$650.56	$619.57	$30.99	$84,938.24
3	$84,938.24	$650.56	$619.34	$31.22	$84,907.02
4	$84,907.02	$650.56	$619.11	$31.45	$84,875.57
5	$84,875.57	$650.56	$618.88	$31.68	$84,843.89
6	$84,843.89	$650.56	$618.65	$31.91	$84,811.98
7	$84,811.98	$650.56	$618.42	$32.14	$84,779.84
8	$84,779.84	$650.56	$618.19	$32.37	$84,747.47
9	$84,747.47	$650.56	$617.95	$32.61	$84,714.86
10	$84,714.86	$650.56	$617.71	$32.85	$84,682.01
11	$84,682.01	$650.56	$617.47	$33.09	$84,648.92
12	$84,648.92	$650.56	$617.23	$33.33	$84,615.59

The total payment during the first year is 12($650.56) = $7806.72. By adding the interest and principal shown in Table 12, we see that the total paid toward interest in the first year is $7422.31, and the total paid toward principal is $384.41. Thus, the percentage of the first year's payments which goes toward interest is

$$\frac{\$7422.31}{\$7806.72} \approx 95.08\% \qquad \text{(toward interest)}$$

and the percentage toward principal is

$$\frac{\$384.41}{\$7806.72} \approx 4.92\%. \qquad \text{(toward principal)}$$ ◆

Try one!

Bob and Norma Jenson take out a home mortgage of $75,000.00 on a new house at 8.25% for 30 years. The monthly payment is $563.45. Construct an amortization schedule for their first year's payments. How much do they pay in the first year? What percentage of this amount goes toward interest? What percentage goes toward principal?

Payment Number	Balance Before Payment	Payment	Interest Payment	Principal Payment	Balance After Payment
1	$75,000.00	$563.45	_____	_____	_____
2	_____	$563.45	_____	_____	_____
3	_____	$563.45	_____	_____	_____
4	_____	$563.45	_____	_____	_____
5	_____	$563.45	_____	_____	_____
6	_____	$563.45	_____	_____	_____
7	_____	$563.45	_____	_____	_____
8	_____	$563.45	_____	_____	_____
9	_____	$563.45	_____	_____	_____
10	_____	$563.45	_____	_____	_____
11	_____	$563.45	_____	_____	_____
12	_____	$563.45	_____	_____	_____

Total paid in first year: _____

Percent toward interest: _____   Percent toward principal: _____

Notice from Table 12 that the interest payment decreases, and the principal payment increases as each successive payment is made. However, for the mortgage in Example 3, it will take many years for the interest payment to drop below the principal payment. By the time this happens, most of the interest for this loan will have been paid. Figure 3 demonstrates this phenomenon graphically. For example, after 15 years of payments, Ruth and Stewart will have made payments totaling $117,100.80. Of this amount, $105,717.01 will have been payment toward interest and only $11,383.79 will have been payment toward principal.

Figure 3

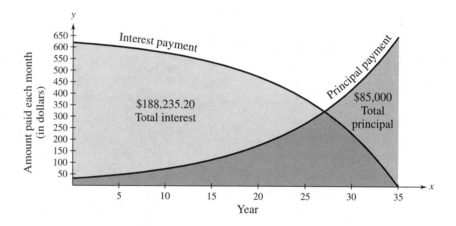

EXAMPLE 4   Reducing the balance by making additional payments

Ruth and Stewart Segal (see Example 3) are both working and decide they can afford to make an additional payment of $353.62 along with their first mortgage payment of $650.56.

a. What will their mortgage balance be after this payment?

b. How much interest did Ruth and Stewart save by making this additional payment?

SOLUTION

Ruth and Stewart made a total payment of

$650.56 + $353.62 = $1004.18.

Of this amount, $619.79 goes toward interest (see Table 13) and therefore, the amount applied toward the principal is

$1004.18 − $619.79 = $384.39.

a. Thus, the balance after this payment is

balance = $85,000.00 − $384.39 = $84,615.61.

b. To find the amount of interest the Segals saved by making this additional payment, we observe from the amortization schedule in Table 12 that Ruth and Stewart would not have reached a balance of approximately $84,615.61 until their 12th regular payment. In other words, the additional payment of $353.62 prepaid the principal for payments 2 through 12 and the Segals *do not have to pay* the corresponding eleven interest payments. This represents an eventual savings of

$619.57 + $619.34 + $619.11

+ ... + $617.47 + $617.23 = $6802.52.   ◆

Try one!

Robin and Thomas Clarke get a $70,000.00 mortgage at 9% for 30 years. The amortization schedule for the first year is given below.

Payment Number	Balance Before Payment	Payment	Interest Payment	Principal Payment	Balance After Payment
1	$70,000.00	$563.24	$525.00	$38.24	$69,961.76
2	$69,961.76	$563.24	$524.71	$38.53	$69,923.23
3	$69,923.23	$563.24	$524.42	$38.82	$69,884.41
4	$69,884.41	$563.24	$524.13	$39.11	$69,845.30
5	$69,845.30	$563.24	$523.84	$39.40	$69,805.90
6	$69,805.90	$563.24	$523.54	$39.70	$69,766.20
7	$69,766.20	$563.24	$523.25	$39.99	$69,726.21
8	$69,726.21	$563.24	$522.95	$40.29	$69,685.92
9	$69,685.92	$563.24	$522.64	$40.60	$69,645.32
10	$69,645.32	$563.24	$522.34	$40.90	$69,604.42
11	$69,604.42	$563.24	$522.03	$41.21	$69,563.21
12	$69,563.21	$563.24	$521.72	$41.52	$69,521.69

Robin and Thomas decided that they can afford to make an additional payment of $440.05 along with their first mortgage payment of $563.24.

a. What will their mortgage balance be after this payment?

b. How much interest did Robin and Thomas save by making this additional payment?

Balance: _____   Interest saved: _____

The value of most houses increases each year. The actual rate of increase depends upon many factors: the rate of inflation, the size and location of the home, the condition and age of the home, and the cost of maintaining the home. When a mortgaged home is sold, the difference between the selling price and the balance due on the mortgage is called the seller's **equity**. In general, a homeowner's equity will increase the longer he or she has the mortgage. However, since the balance on a typical mortgage decreases very slowly during the first several years of the mortgage, the major source of equity increase is the inflating value of the home. The next example describes such a situation.

EXAMPLE 5   Finding the balance due and equity on a home

Sam Davis accepts employment for two years in a new town. He buys a small apartment and incurs the following expenses.

$52,000.00	list price of apartment
+ 2,500.00	closing costs
$54,500.00	
−10,000.00	down payment
$44,500.00	amount financed

Sam finances his mortgage at 9.5% for 30 years, giving him a monthly payment of $374.18. During the two years, Sam pays $730.00 for property taxes, $510.00 for home insurance, $1200.00 for interior improvements, and $680.00 on miscellaneous home repairs and upkeep. At the end of the two years of payments, Sam sells the apartment for $60,000.00 of which he pays 6.5% (or $3900.00) in realtor's commission. What is the balance due at the end of two years? What is the equity? How much did it cost Sam to live in this home for two years?

SOLUTION

We begin by finding Sam's balance after 24 payments.

$$B = \left(1 + \frac{R}{12}\right)^{n}\left(P - \frac{12M}{R}\right) + \frac{12M}{R}$$

$$= \left(1 + \frac{0.095}{12}\right)^{24}\left(\$44,500.00 - \frac{12(\$374.18)}{0.095}\right) + \frac{12(\$374.18)}{0.095}$$

$$\approx \$43,923.96.$$

Sam's equity is

$60,000.00	selling price of home
−43,923.96	balance due on mortgage
$16,076.04	equity

Sam's expenses for buying, maintaining, and selling the home are

$10,000.00	down payment
2,500.00	closing costs
8,980.32	24 payments of $374.18
730.00	property taxes
510.00	home insurance
1,200.00	interior improvements
680.00	home repair
+ 3,900.00	realtor's commission
$28,500.32	expenses for two years

Since Sam spent $28,500.32 in order to build up $16,076.04 in equity, his cost of buying, maintaining, and selling this home is

$28,500.32	expenses for two years
−16,076.04	equity
$12,424.28	cost of buying, maintaining, and selling ◆

Try one!

Kathleen and Tim Burns buy a house for $70,000.00 of which they mortgage $66,500.00 at 8.5% for 30 years, giving them a monthly payment of $511.33. After five years, they sell the house for $85,000.00. What is the balance due at the end of the five years, and what is their equity at the time they sell the house?

Answer: _____   Answer: _____

Sam Davis' situation in Example 5 bears close inspection. Many people in Sam's situation would claim that since they had paid $52,000.00 for a home and sold it for $60,000.00 two years later that they made a profit of $8000.00. In doing so, they neglect to account for all the expenses of buying, maintaining, and selling a home. Of course, Sam did pay a total of $8404.28 in interest and $730.00 in taxes which (assuming a 25% tax bracket) saved him $2283.57 in his income taxes. But, at the same time, had he not purchased the home, he could have invested the $10,000.00 down payment for two years which (assuming 7% compounded continuously) would pay him $1502.74 in interest (of which approximately $375.68 would be paid in income taxes, leaving a profit of $1127.06).

Should Sam have bought or rented? Let's compare his expenses for buying or renting over two years. We'll assume that Sam could have found a comparable apartment to rent for $375.00 per month.

Sam Buys a Home for Two Years		Same Rents for Two Years	
$28,500.32	expenses for buying, maintaining and selling home	$9,000.00	rent of $375.00 per month for two years
		− 200.00	renter's insurance
−16,076.04	equity	$9,200.00	
$12,424.28			interest profit on
− 2,283.57	savings on income tax	−1,127.06	$10,000.00 investment
$10,140.71	net expenses for two years	$8,072.94	net expenses for two years

Does this example mean that it costs more to buy than to rent? Yes, in some cases it does! Of course, there are many situations in which buying is less expensive than renting. The point is that both buying *and* renting are expensive and the advantages of one over the other demand careful consideration. In general, the longer a person plans to live in a home, the more advantageous buying becomes.

Important Terms

A, total loan payment

B, balance due after *n* payments

closing costs

down payment

equity

F, finance charge

home mortgage

I, minimum monthly payment

list price of a home

M, monthly payment

N, number of payments

P, principal

R, annual percentage rate

realtor's commission

term of mortgage

Important Formulas

$$I = PRT = \frac{PR}{12}$$

$$B = \left(1 + \frac{R}{12}\right)^{n}\left(P - \frac{12M}{R}\right) + \frac{12M}{R}$$

CONSUMER HINTS

- When obtaining a home mortgage, set the term for as few years as you can afford. The difference in monthly payments between a 20-year mortgage and a 30-year mortgage is often affordable.

- For short periods of time it may be cheaper to rent than to buy. Realtors make money by selling homes. They are usually not in the renting business and they are certainly not in the financial counseling business. Do not be overly swayed by a realtor's arguments of the advantages of buying over renting.

- If you have a home mortgage and are able to make extra payments, do it. You can save huge amounts of interest by making extra payments that apply directly to the principal of your mortgage.

- The federal government offers various programs to help young home buyers, veterans, financially disabled buyers, or buyers of homes in poor condition. Check with your local federal offices to see if you qualify for help.

SECTION 4   EXERCISES

1. A $76,000.00 home is purchased with a 10% down payment. The remainder of the price of the home plus $3475.00 closing costs is financed with a home mortgage. Find the size of the mortgage.

Answer: _____

2. A $60,000.00 home is purchased with a 15% down payment. The remainder of the price of the home plus $1950.00 closing costs is financed with a home mortgage. Find the size of the mortgage.

Answer: _____

In Exercises 3–8, assume that a home buyer obtains a $70,000.00 mortgage.

3. Find the monthly payment, the total payment and the finance charge if the annual percentage rate is 8% and the term of the mortgage is

    a. 20 years.

                                                                   Monthly Payment: _____

     Total Payment: _____   Finance Charge: _____

    b. 25 years.

                                                                   Monthly Payment: _____

     Total Payment: _____   Finance Charge: _____

    c. 30 years.

                                                                   Monthly Payment: _____

     Total Payment: _____   Finance Charge: _____

    d. 35 years.

                                                                   Monthly Payment: _____

     Total Payment: _____   Finance Charge: _____

4. Find the monthly payment, the total payment and the finance charge if the annual percentage rate is 9% and the term of the mortgage is

a. 20 years.

Monthly Payment: _____

Total Payment: _____   Finance Charge: _____

b. 25 years.

Monthly Payment: _____

Total Payment: _____   Finance Charge: _____

c. 30 years.

Monthly Payment: _____

Total Payment: _____   Finance Charge: _____

d. 35 years.

Monthly Payment: _____

Total Payment: _____   Finance Charge: _____

5. Use the results of Exercise 3 with the monthly payment and finance charges for the 20-year mortgage as the point of comparison to find the percentage decrease in monthly payments and the percentage increase in finance charges when the term is increased to

    a. 25 years.

Percent Decrease: _____   Percent Increase: _____

    b. 30 years.

Percent Decrease: _____   Percent Increase: _____

    c. 35 years.

Percent Decrease: _____   Percent Increase: _____

6. Use the results of Exercise 4 with the monthly payment and finance charges for the 20-year mortgage as the point of comparison to find the percentage decrease in monthly payments and the percentage increase in finance charges when the term is increased to

a. 25 years.

Percent Decrease: _____   Percent Increase: _____

b. 30 years.

Percent Decrease: _____   Percent Increase: _____

c. 35 years.

Percent Decrease: _____   Percent Increase: _____

7. At an annual percentage rate of 9%, what is the minimum monthly payment necessary to pay the interest on the mortgage?

Answer: _____

8. At an annual percentage rate of 11%, what is the minimum monthly payment necessary to pay the interest on the mortgage?

Answer: _____

9. For a home mortgage of $80,000.00 at 8% for 25 years, complete the following table where *n* represents the number of payments.

Time in Years	*n*	Balance Due after *n* Payments	Total of First *n* Payments	Principal Paid after *n* Payments	Interest Paid after *n* Payments
5	60				
10	120				
15	180				
20	240				
25	300				

10. For a home mortgage of $60,000.00 at 10.5% for 35 years, complete the following table where *n* represents the number of payments.

Time in Years	*n*	Balance Due after *n* Payments	Total of First *n* Payments	Principal Paid after *n* Payments	Interest Paid after *n* Payments
5	60	_____	_____	_____	_____
10	120	_____	_____	_____	_____
15	180	_____	_____	_____	_____
20	240	_____	_____	_____	_____
25	300	_____	_____	_____	_____
30	360	_____	_____	_____	_____

11. Victoria Buchanan obtains a home mortgage for $70,000.00 at 9.5% for 25 years. At the end of 3.5 years of regular monthly payments, Victoria has a balance of $67,152.10 on her mortgage. Complete the following amortization schedule for Victoria's mortgage for payments 43 through 48.

Payment Number	Balance before Payment	Payment	Interest Payment	Principal Payment	Balance after Payment
43	$67,152.10	_____	_____	_____	_____
44	_____	_____	_____	_____	_____
45	_____	_____	_____	_____	_____
46	_____	_____	_____	_____	_____
47	_____	_____	_____	_____	_____
48	_____	_____	_____	_____	_____

12. Mark and Cindy Bukowski obtain a home mortgage for $60,000.00 at 10.5% for 35 years. At the end of 4.5 years of regular monthly payments, Mark and Cindy have a balance of $59,047.11 on their mortgage. Complete the following amortization schedule for Mark and Cindy's mortgage for payments 55 through 60.

Payment Number	Balance before Payment	Payment	Interest Payment	Principal Payment	Balance after Payment
55	$59,047.11	_____	_____	_____	_____
56	_____	_____	_____	_____	_____
57	_____	_____	_____	_____	_____
58	_____	_____	_____	_____	_____
59	_____	_____	_____	_____	_____
60	_____	_____	_____	_____	_____

13. Suppose that Victoria Buchanan (see Exercise 11) was able to make an additional payment of $409.44 along with her regular 43rd payment. What would her balance be after making this additional payment? How much interest did Victoria save?

Balance: _____   Savings: _____

14. Suppose that Mark and Cindy Bukowski (see Exercise 12) were able to make an additional payment of $114.05 along with their regular 55th payment. What would their balance be after making this additional payment? How much interest did mark and Cindy save by making this additional payment?

Balance: _____   Savings: _____

15. George Lewis obtains a home mortgage for $50,000.00 at 10.5% for 30 years. What percentage of his first year's payments goes toward the principal? What percentage goes toward interest?

Percent Toward Principal: _____   Percent Toward Interest: _____

16. Denise and Barry Thomas obtain a home mortgage for $50,000.00 at 12% for 20 years. What percentage of their first year's payments goes toward the principal? What percentage goes toward interest?

Percent Toward Principal: _____   Percent Toward Interest: _____

17. Dr. Robert Hutchinson and his wife Carol buy a home for $100,000.00 of which they mortgage $82,500.00 at 9% for 20 years. After three years, they sell the home for $105,900.00. What is their equity at the time they sell the house?

Answer: _____

18. Rita and Ed Orlando bought a small house in 1980 for $48,000.00 of which they mortgaged $45,000.00 at 15% for 30 years. After five years, they sold the house for $69,500.00. What was their equity at the time they sold the house?

Answer: _____

Section 5

Credit Cards

Many consumers would be startled to go into a store to purchase a small item and be asked the question, "Would you like to take out a loan to cover the cost of this purchase?" And yet that is precisely what is being asked by the question "Will this purchase be cash or charge?" When a purchase is *charged*, the buyer is actually taking out a loan for the purchase price.

The most common way to charge items is by the use of a **credit card**. There are literally hundreds of different kinds of credit cards available today, most of which can be classified as one of two basic types. The first type is the **single-purpose** credit card that allows buyers to charge purchases with a particular company such as a department store (Sears, Penney's, Montgomery Ward), an oil company (Exxon, Texaco, Gulf), or a car rental agency (Hertz, Avis, National). The second basic type of credit card is the **multipurpose** credit card (Visa, Master Card, Discover, American Express) that allows buyers to charge a wide variety of purchases with different companies. In addition to charging purchases, the multipurpose card allows its holder to obtain small loans in the form of **cash advances**.

Usually, there is no interest charged on credit card debts for *purchases* that are paid within a month. In this respect, credit cards provide consumers with interest-free, short-term loans. However, interest is charged on cash advances and on purchases that are not paid within a month. When interest is charged, the annual percentage rate normally ranges between 12% and 22%.

> **EXAMPLE 1** **Finding the monthly finance charge on past due balance**

Robert Schultz received the following statement for gasoline charges.

Previous Balance $84.20	Statement Date October 5
Payments Received $84.20	Date of Last Payment September 24
Past Due Balance ——	Finance Charge ——
New Purchases $87.90	New Balance $87.90

Finance Charge is on Past Due Balance
at the rate of
1.25% Monthly Rate
15% Annual Percentage Rate

*To avoid finance charges, the new
balance must be received before the
next statement date: November 5*

a. How much did Robert charge on this credit card in the billing period covered by this statement?

b. If Robert neglects to pay before the next billing date, what would his past due balance be on November 5th and what would the finance charge be?

SOLUTION

a. Robert's charges since the last billing date total $87.90.

b. If Robert does not pay the $87.90 by November 5, his past due balance will be $87.90 and he will be assessed a finance charge of

$$F = PRT = (\$87.90)(0.15)\left(\tfrac{1}{12}\right)$$

$$= (\$87.90)(0.0125)*$$

$$\approx \$1.10.$$

*Note that the **monthly rate** is computed by dividing the annual percentage rate by 12 no matter how many days are in the actual billing period.

Try one!

Susan Lubold received the following statement for department store charges.

Previous Balance $105.23	Statement Date April 10
Payments Received $105.23	Date of Last Payment March 25
Past Due Balance ——	Finance Charge ——
New Purchases $159.95	New Balance $159.95

Finance Charge is on Past Due Balance
at the rate of
1.5% Monthly Rate
18% Annual Percentage Rate

*To avoid finance charges, the new
balance must be received before the
next statement date: May 10*

a. How much did Susan charge on this credit card in the billing period covered by this statement?

b. If Susan neglects to pay before the next billing date, what would her past due balance be on May 10th and what would the finance charge be?

Answer **a**: _____   Answer **b**: _____

There are three basic methods for calculating the finance charge on credit card accounts: the unpaid balance method, the average daily balance method, and the average daily balance with unpaid balance method.

The **unpaid balance method** (see Example 1) is the oldest of these three types and requires the least amount of bookkeeping. With this method, finance charges are not computed on purchases that are paid within one month of billing. Thus, as long as the cardholder pays the total balance each month, there is no finance charge. Most companies that use this method attempt to discourage unpaid balances on their accounts. The unpaid balance is often called a *past due balance* and the credit card holder is specifically asked to pay in full each month. If the past due balance is allowed to linger, the cardholder is usually asked to stop charging until the unpaid balance is paid.

The second method of computing finance charges is called the **average daily balance method**. To find the average daily balance *ADB* between two billing dates, the balances for each day in the billing period are added together and this total is divided by the number of days in the billing period.

$$ADB = \frac{\frac{\text{Balance}}{\text{Day 1}} + \frac{\text{Balance}}{\text{Day 2}} + \cdots + \frac{\text{Balance}}{\text{Day } N}}{N}$$

With this method, the finance charges are incurred from the date the charge is entered into the account, and the cardholder must pay a finance charge even if the account is paid in full within a month (see Example 4). Of course, the longer the account is unpaid, the larger the finance charge. All cash advances on credit cards use this method of computing finance charges.

The third method of computing finance charges on credit card accounts is called the **average daily with unpaid balance method** (see Example 3). This method is actually a combination of the first two methods. It is like the unpaid balance method in that as long as the account is paid in full each month, there is no finance charge. However, for any month that the account is not paid in full, the billing method switches to the average daily balance method. This method of computing finance charges was started by the major bank cards (Visa and Master Card) and is becoming, for purchases, the most common of the three methods.

Since the balance of an account changes only when a purchase, credit, or payment is recorded, the average daily balance is usually calculated by dividing the billing period into blocks of time corresponding to the changes in the balance. For instance, if (in a 31-day billing period) the balance of an account was $250.00 for 13 days, $100.00 for eight days, and $175.00 for ten days, the average daily balance would be

$$ADB = \frac{13(\$250.00) + 8(\$100.00) + 10(\$175.00)}{31}$$

$$\approx \$187.10.$$

EXAMPLE 2   Finding the average daily balance

Kimberly Rossi received the following credit card statement.

Record of Payments and Purchases		
1/11	Ocean View Restaurant	$39.80
1/16	Payment – Thank You	$200.00–
2/5	Clark's Stereo Shop	$112.14

Previous Billing Date: 1/8	*Current Billing Date:* 2/8

Previous Purchase Balance: $340.78	Monthly Rate 1.50%
Previous Finance Charge: $5.60	Annual Percentage Rate 18%
Previous Total Balance: $346.38	

To avoid **FINANCE CHARGES** on New Balance of Purchases, pay the full amount thereof by Date Payment Due. If not so paid, **FINANCE CHARGES** will be incurred on the Average Daily Balance of Purchases.

a. What is Kimberly's average daily balance for this billing period?

b. What is the finance charge for this billing period?

SOLUTION

We begin by constructing a record of Kimberly's daily balance as shown in Table 13.

TABLE 13

Date	Purchase	Payment toward Purchase	Payment toward Finance Charge	Purchase Balance	Number of Days
1/9	—	—	—	$340.78	2
1/11	$39.80	—	—	$380.58	5
1/16	—	$194.40	$5.60	$186.18	20
2/5	$112.14	—	—	$298.32	4
			Days in Billing Period =		31

Note that only $194.40 of Kimberly's payment is applied toward the purchase balance; the remaining $5.60 is used to cover the previous month's finance charge.

a. Now, we can use Table 13 to find the average daily balance:

$$ADB = \frac{2(\$340.78) + 5(\$380.58) + 20(\$186.18) + 4(\$298.32)}{31}$$

$$\approx \$241.98$$

b. The finance charge is

$$F = (\text{Average Daily Balance})(\text{Monthly Rate})$$

$$= (\$241.98)(0.015)$$

$$\approx \$3.63.$$ ◆

EXAMPLE 2a

Steps	Display
2 $\times$ 340.78 $+$	681.56
5 $\times$ 380.58 $+$	2584.46
20 $\times$ 186.18 $+$	6308.06
4 $\times$ 298.32 $=$	7501.34
$\div$ 31 $=$	241.9787097

Try one!

Bob Martin received the following credit card statement.

Record of Payments and Purchases		
1/11	Fisherman's Net Restaurant	$45.60
1/16	Payment – Thank You	$250.00–
2/5	Nick's Bicycle Shop	$175.29

Previous Billing Date: 1/8	*Current Billing Date:* 2/8
Previous Purchase Balance: $360.49 Previous Finance Charge: $5.41 Previous Total Balance: $365.90	Monthly Rate 1.50% --- Annual Percentage Rate 18%

To avoid **FINANCE CHARGES** on New Balance of Purchases, pay the full amount thereof by Date Payment Due. If not so paid, **FINANCE CHARGES** will be incurred on the Average Daily Balance of Purchases.

a. What is Bob's average daily balance for this billing period?

b. What is the finance charge for this billing period?

Answer **a**: _____   Answer **b**: _____

EXAMPLE 3	**Finding the finance charge: average daily with unpaid balance method**

Kirk and Debbie Parrish are in the habit of paying their credit card balance in full each month to avoid finance charges. When writing out the payment check one month, Kirk mistakenly made the check out for $198.69 rather than the actual total balance of $198.96. During the next month, Kirk and Debbie had an average daily balance of $247.68. How much did Kirk's error cost the couple in finance charges? (Assume the finance charges are computed with the average daily with unpaid balance method at a monthly rate of 1.25%.)

SOLUTION

The unpaid balance on next month's statement is

$198.96   previous balance
−198.69   payment
$0.27   unpaid balance

Since the account has an unpaid balance, the finance charge is based on the average daily balance (without the benefit of a one month grace period). Since the 27¢ is already accounted for in the average daily balance, the finance charge is

$$F = \text{(Average Daily Balance)(Monthly Rate)}$$

$$= (\$247.68)(0.0125)$$

$$\approx \$3.10$$

Note that if Kirk had left no unpaid balance (in other words, he had paid the balance in full) the finance charge would have been zero. Thus, Kirk's 27¢ error cost $3.10.   ◆

Example 3 demonstrates the disadvantage (for consumers) of the average daily with unpaid balance method as compared with the unpaid balance method. Using the unpaid balance method, Kirk would have been required to pay a finance charge only on the unpaid balance of 27¢.

Try one!

Bob and Lynne Withers are in the habit of paying their credit card balance in full each month to avoid finance charges. This month, Bob mistakenly paid only $254.49 rather than the actual total balance of $254.94. During the next month, Bob and Lynne had an average daily balance of $235.75. How much did this error cost Bob and Lynn in finance charges? (Assume the finance charges are computed with the average daily with unpaid balance method at a monthly rate of 1.5%.)

Answer: _____

| EXAMPLE 4 | Finding the finance charge: average daily balance method |

Kathleen Sweeny took out two cash advances: $500.00 on April 1 and $400.00 on April 10. Her monthly billing dates were March 27 and April 26. Find the finance charge on the April 26th statement. (Assume Kathleen had no previous balance and the finance charge is based on the average daily balance at a monthly rate of 1%.)

SOLUTION

During this billing period, Kathleen's account had the balances shown below.

Date	Cash Advance	Balance	Number of Days
3/28	—	$0.00	4
4/1	$500.00	$500.00	9
4/10	$400.00	$900.00	17
		Days in Billing Period =	30

Thus, the average daily balance is

$$ADB = \frac{4(\$0.00) + 9(\$500.00) + 17(\$900.00)}{30}$$

$$= \$660.00$$

and the finance charge is

$$F = (\$660.00)(0.01) = \$6.60.$$ ◆

Try one!

Judy Strickler took out two cash advances: $400.00 on September 1 and $300.00 on September 10. Her monthly billing dates were August 27 and September 26. Find the finance charge on the September 26th statement. (Assume Judy had no previous balance and the finance charge is based on the average daily balance at a monthly rate of 1.25%.)

Answer: _____

In all three methods of computing finance charges, a monthly payment is required. For the unpaid balance method, the required monthly payment is usually the total balance due. This is considered a disadvantage by many consumers since it may involve a sizable amount of money one month and very little (or nothing) the next. Many cardholders prefer to extend the repayment schedule of sizable purchases (or cash advances) over several months by making **minimum monthly payments**. This type of repayment schedule is normally offered by the two methods that use average daily balances in the calculation of finance charges. The minimum monthly payment is based upon a percentage of the balance of the account. The actual percentage used to compute the minimum required payment usually varies from 3% to 10% depending on the company issuing the credit card.

EXAMPLE 5 — Finding the balance after making minimum payments

Keith Branton belongs to a labor union that went on strike. Keith had just charged $450.00 on a credit card and was planning to pay the full amount when the statement arrived. After the strike began, Keith decided to make minimum monthly payments until he went back to work. After the fifth minimum payment, the strike ended and Keith was able to pay the remaining balance on the sixth payment. If the minimum payment required was 5% of the total unpaid balance and the finance charge was 1.25% monthly, how much finance charge did Keith have to pay? (Assume there are no other charges and no finance charge the first month.)

SOLUTION

For the first month, the minimum payment was 5% of $450.00 or

First Month's Payment = ($450.00)(0.05) = $22.50.

For the second month, the total unpaid balance was

$427.50   balance after payment
− 5.34   finance charge of 1.25% on $427.50
$432.84   total unpaid balance

The minimum payment due on this balance was

Second Month's Payment = ($432.84)(0.05) ≈ $21.64.

To find the balance after five minimum payments, we continue this procedure and obtain the results shown in Table 14.

TABLE 14 — PURCHASE BALANCE RECORD

Payment Number	Finance Charge	Balance before Payment	Payment	Balance after Payment
1	—*	$450.00	$22.50	$427.50
2	$5.34	$432.84	$21.64	$411.20
3	$5.14	$416.34	$20.82	$395.52
4	$4.94	$400.46	$20.02	$380.44
5	$4.76	$385.20	$19.26	$365.94
6	$4.57	$370.51	$370.51	—
	Total: $24.75		Total: $474.75	

*One month grace period

Thus, Keith's finance charge over the six-month period totaled $24.75.   ◆

Try one!

Suppose that the strike (from Example 5) ended after the eighth payment rather than after the fifth, and Keith paid the remaining balance on the ninth payment instead of the sixth. How much additional finance charge did Keith have to pay?

Answer: _____

EXAMPLE 6   **Comparing finance charges on cash advances and purchases**

In Example 5, Keith Branton made payments on a purchase charge of $450.00 over a six-month period. Suppose that instead, Keith had taken out a $450.00 cash advance (on another credit card) 25 days after he was billed for the $450.00 and used the advance to pay off the purchase balance on the first card. If Keith makes minimum payments of 5% of the total unpaid balance on the cash advance and is able to pay off the balance in the sixth month, how much did he pay in finance charges? (Assume that the monthly rate on cash advances is 1%.)

SOLUTION

Since Keith used the cash advance to pay the purchase balance within a month of its billing, he had no finance charge on purchases. Furthermore, since Keith didn't take the cash advance until roughly one month had gone by, he has only five (instead of six) months to make payments on the cash advance. The record of Keith's cash advance payments is shown in Table 15. (For convenience, we assume that the cash advance was taken out on the first day of the billing period of Keith's second credit card.)

TABLE 15 BALANCE RECORD

Payment Number	Finance Charge	Balance before Payment	Payment	Balance after Payment
Purchase Balance Record (Card 1)				
1	—	$450.00	$450.00	—
Cash Advance Balance Record (Card 2)				
1	$4.50*	$454.50	$22.73	$431.77
2	$4.32	$436.09	$21.80	$414.29
3	$4.14	$418.43	$20.92	$397.51
4	$3.98	$401.49	$20.07	$381.42
5	$3.81	$385.23	$385.23	—
Total: $20.75			Total: $470.75	

*No grace period on cash advances

From Table 14 in Example 5, we see that the total finance charge is $24.75, whereas in Table 15, the total finance charge is $20.75. Thus, by taking out a cash advance *after* taking advantage of the one-month's grace period on purchases, Keith saved

$$\$24.75 - \$20.75 = \$4.00$$

in finance charges.   ◆

The reason multipurpose credit cards can afford to give a month's grace period on purchases is that the card issuer (the bank, credit union, savings and loan association, etc.) receives a 2% to 8% fee called a **merchant discount**, on every credit card purchase. In other words, if you charge $100.00 on your bank credit card at the local hardware store, the bank issuing the card keeps a percentage of the $100.00 and returns the remainder to the hardware store. While this percentage does not appear directly on the cardholder's receipts, it does appear indirectly in the form of higher retail prices. Because of the fact that they do not receive the full price for items charged on bank credit cards, some retailers offer discounts for customers who are willing to pay cash.

> **EXAMPLE 7**   **Finding the annual percentage rate including merchant discount**

Laura Crestwood charged $197.00 on her bank card on November 11 at the Liberty Furniture Store. On November 20, the charge was posted by the bank into Laura's account and the Liberty Furniture Store's account was credited with $187.15 (the $197.00 charge less a 5% merchant discount of $9.85). On December 10, Laura was billed by the bank. On January 5, Laura paid her account in full. Assuming that Laura had an unpaid balance on December 10, part of Laura's payment would have included $1.72 finance charge on the $197.00 purchase. Find the annual percentage rate *received by the bank* for their outlay of $187.15.

SOLUTION

The bank paid out $187.15 on November 20 and received

$$\$197.00 + \$1.72 = \$198.72$$

on January 5. This means that the bank received

$$\$198.72 - \$187.15 = \$11.57$$

in interest for a 46-day loan of $187.15. The annual percentage rate for such a loan is

$$R = \frac{\$11.57}{(\$187.15)\left(\frac{46}{365}\right)} \approx 0.4905 = 49.05\%.$$

Note that if Laura had paid her account on December 15, the bank would have received $11.57 interest for a 25-day loan of $187.15. The annual percentage rate in this case would be

$$R = \frac{F}{PT} = \frac{\$11.57}{(\$187.15)\left(\frac{25}{365}\right)} \approx 0.9026 = 90.26\%.$$

No wonder banks are eager to get their customers to use credit cards! ◆

Try one!

Carla Robinson charged $149.00 on her bank card on September 11 at the Cook's Gallery Gourmet Shop. On September 20, the charge was posted by the bank into Carla's account and the Cook's Gallery Gourmet Shop's account was credited with $146.02 (the $149.00 charge less a 2% merchant discount of $2.98). On October 10, Carla was billed by the bank. On November 5, Carla paid her account in full. Assuming that Carla had an unpaid balance on October 10, part of Carla's payment would have included $1.30 finance charge on the $149.00 purchase. Find the annual percentage rate *received by the bank* for their outlay of $146.02.

Answer: _____

Important Terms

annual percentage rate	merchant discount
average daily balance method	minimum payment
average daily with unpaid balance method	*N*, number of days in billing period
cash advance	multipurpose credit card
F, finance charge	single purpose credit card
grace period	unpaid balance method

Important Formulas

$$ADB = \frac{\frac{Balance}{Day\ 1} + \frac{Balance}{Day\ 2} + \cdots + \frac{Balance}{Day\ N}}{N}$$

For unpaid balance method:
   $F = $ (unpaid balance)(monthly rate)

For average daily balance:
   $F = $ (average daily balance)(monthly rate)

CONSUMER HINTS

- Credit card policies and charges vary from one card issuer to another. For example, two banks offering VISA credit cards may set different policies and charges for their cardholders. When shopping for a credit card, look for the following features:

   1. Interest-free grace period on purchases
   2. No annual membership fee
   3. No minimum monthly finance charge
   4. Low annual percentage rate.

- When possible, avoid finance charges by paying for all purchases after the first billing.

- Ask retailers who accept credit cards if they give discounts to cash customers. If they do not, you may as well charge your purchase and keep your money for another 30 to 60 days in an interest-earning checking account.

- Credit cards can be a wonderful convenience *if* you purchase only those items you would normally have purchased for cash. Studies show that this is seldom the case. For many people, the ability to charge items ultimately results in strained (if not broken) budgets.

- If you lose a credit card, notify the issuer immediately to avoid liability for unauthorized charges.

SECTION 5   EXERCISES

1. Find the average daily balance for a billing period of 30 days if the balance was $135.00 for five days, $205.96 for 18 days, and $105.96 for seven days.

Answer: _____

2. Find the average daily balance for a billing period of 30 days if the balance was $105.76 for eight days, $208.14 for 14 days, $227.56 for five days, and $197.56 for three days.

Answer: _____

3. Find the average daily balance for a billing period of 31 days if the balance was $17.45 for nine days, $423.15 for 16 days, $145.68 for four days, and $197.56 for three days.

Answer: _____

4. Find the average daily balance for a billing period of 31 days if the balance was $17.45 for nine days, $145.68 for 16 days, $213.07 for four days, and $423.15 for two days.

Answer: _____

5. Assume that the account in Exercise 1 is subject to a finance charge on the average daily balance. What is the finance charge for this billing period if the annual percentage rate is

a. 15%?

Answer: _____

b. 18%?

Answer: _____

6. Assume that the account in Exercise 2 is subject to a finance charge on the average daily balance. What is the finance charge for this billing period if the annual percentage rate is

a. 15%?

Answer: _____

b. 18%?

Answer: _____

7. Assume that the following average daily balances are subject to a finance charge of 15% (annual percentage rate). What is the finance charge for a monthly billing period if the average daily balance is

a. $135.68?

Answer: _____

b. $367.45?

Answer: _____

c. $839.05?

Answer: _____

d. $1543.07?

Answer: _____

8. Assume that the following average daily balances are subject to a finance charge of 18% (annual percentage rate). What is the finance charge for a monthly billing period if the average daily balance is

a. $135.68?

Answer: _____

b. $367.45?

Answer: _____

c. $839.05?

Answer: _____

d. $1543.07?

Answer: _____

9. Richard and Arlene Snyder had two unexpected repair bills in October: one for their car and the other for their furnace. To pay for these repairs, Richard and Arlene took out two cash advances: $250.00 on October 8 and $150.00 on October 18. If the Snyders' billing dates are September 28 and October 28, find the finance charge on their October statement using their average daily balance with a monthly rate of 1.25%. (Assume their account had no previous balance.)

Answer: _____

10. William O'Neil took out a cash advance of $300.00 on December 12 for vacation travel expenses. Using the average daily balance with a monthly rate of 1.5%, find the finance charge on William's December statement if his billing dates are November 27 and December 27. (Assume the account had no previous balance.)

Answer: _____

11. Suppose that Robert Schultz (see Example 1 of this section) paid $50.00 toward his balance of $87.90 before November 5. Robert's November 5 statement included $108.40 in new purchases.

    a. What is the finance charge on Robert's November 5 statement?

Answer: _____

    b. What is the new balance on Robert's November 5 statement?

Answer: _____

12. Suppose that Robert Schultz's new purchases (see Exercise 11) were entered into his account as follows: $15.50 on October 10, $75.40 on October 15, and $17.50 on November 1. If the finance charges are calculated using the average daily with unpaid balance method (instead of the unpaid balance method as in Exercise 11) how much finance charge would appear on Robert's November 5 statement? (As in Exercise 11, use a monthly rate of 1.25% and an unpaid balance of $37.90.)

Answer: _____

13. Al and Jean Delany purchased a new refrigerator that cost $750.00 and charged the purchase on their credit card. They plan to pay this debt by making minimum monthly payments of 10% of the unpaid balance. Assuming that the finance charge is 1.25% per month on the unpaid balance with no finance charge the first month, construct a payment schedule showing the first five payments.

Payment Number	Finance Charge	Balance before Payment	Payment	Balance after Payment
1	_____	_____	_____	_____
2	_____	_____	_____	_____
3	_____	_____	_____	_____
4	_____	_____	_____	_____
5	_____	_____	_____	_____
Total: _____			Total: _____	

14. Steve Taylor charged $500.00 in purchases on his credit card. He plans to make minimum monthly payments of 8% on the unpaid balance for four months and pay the remainder on the fifth payment. Assuming that the finance charge is 1.5% per month on the unpaid balance with no finance charge the first month, construct a payment schedule showing Steve's five payments.

Payment Number	Finance Charge	Balance before Payment	Payment	Balance after Payment
1	_____	_____	_____	_____
2	_____	_____	_____	_____
3	_____	_____	_____	_____
4	_____	_____	_____	_____
5	_____	_____	_____	_____
Total: _____			Total: _____	

15. Fred Keister buys four new tires for $372.00 and charges the purchase on his credit card. If this charge is subject to a 6% merchant's discount, how much of this amount will the tire dealer receive? (Ignore any sales tax.)

Answer: _____

16. Linda Phelps charged a $739.00 couch on her credit card. If Linda's charge was subject to a merchant's discount of 4%, how much of this amount will the dealer actually receive? (Ignore any sales tax.)

Answer: _____

17. On July 13, at a local department store, Robert Tanner charged $379.00 on his bank credit card. On July 18, the charge was posted by the bank into Robert's account and the department store was credited with $360.05 (merchant's discount). On August 6, Robert paid his account in full. Assuming Robert had no unpaid balance in his account, find the annual percentage rate received by the bank for their outlay of $360.05.

Answer: _____

18. Rebecca Mace charged $231.95 on her credit card on March 29 for the repair of her car at a local garage. On April 8, the charge was posted by the bank into Rebecca's account and the garage was credited with $222.67 (merchant's discount). On May 1, Rebecca paid her account in full. Assuming that Rebecca had no unpaid balance in her account, find the annual percentage rate received by the bank for their outlay of $222.67.

Answer: _____

Section 6
Spotlight on the Credit Clerk

Sometime in your life you may find yourself applying for credit in some form or another, whether it be for a home mortgage, a car loan, the purchase of a major appliance or furniture, or simply for a credit card. In all of these situations your application will cross the desk of a credit clerk, sometimes called a credit authorizer.

The credit clerk reviews an applicant's credit history and researches information that determines whether that applicant is creditworthy. These clerks also contact applicants and credit bureaus, as well as other references in order to insure that the records are complete and accurate before approving a loan or line of credit.

You can find credit clerks in a variety of locations, namely banks, mortgage lenders, retail establishments, and credit bureaus. Bank credit clerks primarily process loan and credit card applications, and sometimes prepare loan application packages for underwriters' review. These bank clerks review the applications, order credit reports, and they may also contact employers and references in order to verify income and personal information. When processing mortgages, closing clerks will order appraisals, secure tax forms and bank statements, and prepare the necessary documents for real estate settlements. Sometimes, information found on credit reports or applications appears inaccurate or incomplete and it is the job of the clerk to investigate these situations. Finally, once the loan has been approved, the closing clerk will see to it that all documentation is complete and accurate, that it has been signed by the appropriate parties, that the proper insurance has been purchased, and finally that the applicant has met all necessary terms and conditions of the loan.

Retail establishments quickly approve charges on a customer's account by checking the customer's existing account information.

131

This is usually done automatically on a computer by a salesperson. If no problems show up in the computer, credit is approved; however, if an account shows past due, overextended, invalid, stolen, or if personal information is out-of-date, then the individual making the sale can refer the transaction to a credit authorizer, often located in a store's central office. Out-of-date information can easily be updated by the credit authorizer, but if there is a problem with the credit history, the authorizer must investigate the customer's credit records and payment history in order to decide whether to approve the new charges.

Clerks in credit bureaus gather, update, and verify all the information found in an individual's personal credit report. These clerks are sometimes called credit investigators. These personal credit reports list all of an individual's credit cards, car loans, and other lines of credit along with payment histories for each. It is noted on these reports whether payments were made on time, the balance due, and monthly payment for each of these accounts. These are the reports that the previously mentioned credit clerks use in determining if customers should be permitted to establish new lines of credit.

Credit clerks usually work a 40-hour week. However, sometimes business is particularly busy and the clerk can expect to work overtime. Depending on which type of credit clerk you are, the busy times occur at different times of the year. For real estate, spring and summer are particularly busy since this is when most people buy homes. Credit authorizers in retail establishments are often busier during the holiday shopping seasons and on special sale days. (Sometimes credit clerks will even sit in the entry of a department store, ready and waiting to take a new customer's application!) Authorizers and some clerks sit for long periods of time and often spend many hours in front of a computer terminal. It is therefore important to watch out for potential eyestrain or headache.

For an entry-level position as a credit clerk, you need no special training unless you plan on working as a loan closer or interviewer. These clerks are usually required to have previous work experience in a financial institution, and it is preferred that they have some knowledge of underwriting procedures. Training is usually done on-the-job. There are courses available at vocational schools, colleges and universities, and even in some banks. As a worker gains competence, advancement is possible. You can be promoted to team leader, supervisor, underwriter, loan officer or even to management. Generally speaking, the institutions prefer that applicants for management positions have a bachelor's degree in some business related field, or at least some college-level coursework.

It is important that a credit clerk have excellent communication skills. These jobs require a great deal of telephone contact. Additionally, a credit clerk must have good organizational skills and superior attention to detail. Computer skills and quick, accurate typing are also necessary.

As a credit clerk, earnings will vary depending on the type of clerk you are and the amount of experience you have. Part-time clerks may begin at a minimum hourly wage, but full-time loan closers can earn as much at $25,000 or more per year plus benefits. There were about 258,000 clerks and authorizers employed in 1994 and little change is expected in the employment of credit clerks over the next several years. Job outlook is largely affected by changes in the economy.

If you would like more information about becoming a credit clerk or authorizer, contact your local bank, retail store or credit reporting agency.

SECTION 6   EXERCISES

1. You are the credit clerk in a large furniture store that is having a semi-annual sale. A customer named Mr. Calvert has been referred to the credit department to secure a promissory note. The couch Mr. Calvert wants to buy costs $849.00 and he signs a 90-day note for which he agrees to pay the full amount plus interest calculated at 15% per year. If, in addition to interest there is a $15.00 service charge, what is the actual annual percentage rate of Mr. Calvert's loan?

Answer: _____

2. Your bank lends $2500.00 to Mrs. Landers, a regular customer, for one year at 8% discounted interest. Mrs. Landers was sent to you because she had two questions about her loan. First, she asked "What is the finance charge for this loan?" and second, "What is the annual percentage rate of this loan?" What are the answers to these two questions?

Finance Charge: _____   Annual Percentage Rate: _____

3. In order to prepare a statement in compliance with the Truth-In-Lending Law, you are asked to calculate the finance charge and the annual percentage rate for Mr. Bowers' promissory note of $5000.00 for 90-days at 9% annual interest (Bankers Rule). What are these two values?

Finance Charge: _____   Annual Percentage Rate: _____

4. Mr. and Mrs. Palmer come into the bank where you are a credit clerk. The Palmers applied for an installment loan of $2300.00 to be repaid in 18 monthly payments with an annual percentage rate of 12%. You have checked their credit history and determined that the Palmers are creditworthy, but before they sign the papers you have to determine the monthly payment, the total payment, and the finance charge. What are these three values?

Monthly Payment: _____

Total Payment: _____

Finance Charge: _____

5. You are the credit authorizer for a large car dealership. The salesman brings his customer, Mr. Blanton, to you to apply for a car loan. The base price for the car Mr. Blanton selected is $14,659.00. Additional charges include cruise control, $215.00; leather interior, $435.00; rear window defroster, $189.00; destination charge, $395.00. The salesman tells you that Mr. Blanton's current car has a trade-in value of $5,600.00 and that he is planning on making a down payment of $2000.00. If the closing cost is $40.00, the registration fee is $50.00, and if, in your state, 6% sales tax is calculated on the price of the car after trade-in, how much will Mr. Blanton be financing?

Answer: _____

6. You are one of two credit authorizers in a particular car dealership. The other authorizer has an emergency at home and asks you to finish the authorization she has just started for Mr. and Mrs. Baker. They just bought a car for which they will finance $11,350.00. While discussing the terms of the loan, you find out that the Bakers would like to pay back the car loan over five years. What will the Bakers' monthly payment be if the annual percentage rate for this loan is 8.5%? After hearing the monthly payment amount, the Bakers ask you how much interest they will have paid at the end of the loan period. What do you tell them?

Monthly Payment: _____   Total Payment: _____

7. One day you get a telephone call from Susan Williams, a customer who, two years ago, financed $12,000.00 for four years at 7% when buying a new car. Susan is graduating from college this year and as a graduation gift her father has offered to pay off the balance of her car loan since she worked her way through college and paid her own tuition. Susan wants to know what that balance will be. What do you tell her? (Assume that Susan has made exactly two years' worth of payments.)

Answer: _____

8. As a mortgage credit authorizer, it is your job to meet with families that want to secure a home mortgage. The Johnstons have just purchased a $72,000.00 home with a 5% down payment. The Johnstons wish to finance the remainder of the price of the home plus $2200.00 in closing costs for 30 years. The current interest rate is 8.75%. Find the size of the mortgage and the monthly mortgage payment.

Size of Mortgage: _____   Monthly Payment: _____

9. You work in the customer service section of a mortgage company as a credit clerk. It is your job to answer customer inquiries. Mr. Blakely calls to find out the amount of equity he has in his home since he is considering taking out a home equity loan to do some improvements. If Mr. Blakely's mortgage amount was $65,000.00 for 30 years at 9% and he has made 125 payments, what is his equity?

Answer: _____

10. You work for a credit card company in the customer service section. It has been a long day and just as you get a phone call from a very upset customer, your computer goes down. The customer is very concerned because he feels that there has been an error made in the calculation of his average daily balance and finance charge. All you have to do this is your calculator and the following information provided by the customer:

Billing period: 30 days
$159.25 balance for 6 days
$329.37 balance for 18 days
$175.00 balance for 6 days.

Calculate the customer's average daily balance and finance charge if the average daily balance is subject to an annual percentage rate of 18%.

Average Daily Balance: _____   Finance Charge: _____

Solutions to "Try one!" Exercises

SECTION 1

Page 3

Since there are 24 equal payments of $74.20, the total amount due for this loan is

Total Amount Due $= (24)($74.20) = $1780.80.$

The loan proceeds are found by adding the cost of the computer to the 6% sales tax:

Loan Proceeds $= $1599.99 + ($1599.99)(0.06)$

$\approx $1599.99 + 96.00

$= $1695.99.$

Finally, the cost of credit for this loan is

Cost of Credit $=$ Total Amount Due $-$ Loan Proceeds

$= $1780.80 - 1695.99

$= $84.81.$

Page 5

The amount financed is

$47.35	insurance charges
+ 759.56	loan proceeds
$806.91	amount financed

The total amount due is

$806.91	amount financed
+ 197.46	finance charge
$1004.37	total amount due

Page 8

24	days remaining in April
31	days in May
30	days in June
+ 5	days in July
90	days

The note is due on July 5, 1996.

The amount financed is $5000.00.

Furthermore, the finance charge is

$117.12	interest
+ 30.00	service charge
$147.12	finance charge

Finally, since $T = \frac{90}{365}$, the annual percentage rate is

$$R = \frac{F}{PT} = \frac{\$147.12}{(\$5000.00)\left(\frac{90}{365}\right)} \approx 11.9\%.$$

Page 10

If we let $r = 0.13$ and $t = \frac{90}{360}$, then the finance charge for 90 days is

$$F = Prt = (\$3500.00)(0.13)\left(\frac{90}{360}\right) = \$113.75.$$

Now, to find the annual percentage rate, we let $T = \frac{90}{365}$ and obtain

$$R = \frac{F}{PT} = \frac{\$113.75}{(\$3500.00)\left(\frac{90}{365}\right)} \approx 0.1318 = 13.18\%.$$

Page 12

a. From the given information, we have $P = \$950.00$, $r = 0.1375$, and $T = \frac{60}{365}$. Therefore, the finance charge is

$$F = \frac{P}{1 - rT} - P = \frac{\$950.00}{1 - (0.1375)\left(\frac{60}{365}\right)} - \$950.00 \approx \$21.97.$$

b. The annual percentage rate for this loan is

$$R = \frac{F}{PT} = \frac{\$21.97}{(\$950.00)\left(\frac{60}{365}\right)} \approx 0.1407 = 14.07\%.$$

Page 14

If the loan is taken out on November 5, 1996 for six months, then it would be due on May 5, 1997. The number of days between these two dates is

25	days remaining in November
31	days in December
31	days in January
28	days in February
31	days in March
30	days in April
+ 5	days in May
181	days.

Therefore, the time is $T = \frac{181}{365}$ and the finance charge is

$$F = PRT = (\$3500.00)(0.1875)\left(\tfrac{181}{365}\right) \approx \$325.43.$$

SECTION 2

Page 28

$P = \$2500.00$, $R = 0.115$, and $N = 18$.

$$M = (\$2500.00)\left[\dfrac{\dfrac{0.115}{12}}{1 - \left(\dfrac{1}{\dfrac{0.115}{12} + 1}\right)^{18}}\right] \approx \$151.88$$

Total payment $= 18(\$151.88) = \$2733.84$.

Page 30

$P = \$4000.00$, $R = 0.065$, and $N = 60$.

$$M = (\$4000.00)\left[\dfrac{\dfrac{0.065}{12}}{1 - \left(\dfrac{1}{\dfrac{0.065}{12} + 1}\right)^{60}}\right] \approx \$78.26$$

Total payment $= 60(\$78.26) = \$4695.60$.

Finance charge $=$ total payment $-$ principal $= \$4695.60 - \$4000.00 = \$695.60$.

Page 32

$P = \$315.00$, $R = 0.13$, and $N = 12$.

$$M = (\$315.00)\left[\dfrac{\dfrac{0.13}{12}}{1 - \left(\dfrac{1}{\dfrac{0.13}{12} + 1}\right)^{12}}\right] \approx \$28.13$$

Page 36

$P = \$1000.00$, $R = 0.095$, and $N = 6$.

$$M = (\$1000.00)\left[\dfrac{\dfrac{0.095}{12}}{1 - \left(\dfrac{1}{\dfrac{0.095}{12} + 1}\right)^{6}}\right] \approx \$171.32$$

Payment Number	Balance Before Payment	Payment	Interest Payment	Principal Payment	Balance After Payment
1	$1000.00	$171.32	$7.92	$163.40	$836.60
2	$836.60	$171.32	$6.62	$164.70	$671.90
3	$671.90	$171.32	$5.32	$166.00	$505.90
4	$505.90	$171.32	$4.01	$167.31	$338.59
5	$338.59	$171.32	$2.68	$168.64	$169.95
6	$169.95	$171.30*	$1.35	$169.95	$0.00

*Sum of balance before payment and interest payment slightly less than monthly monthly payment due to rounding.

Page 38

$A = NM = (18)(\$153.62) = \$2765.16$

$F = A - P = \$2765.16 - \$2500.00 = \$265.16$

First six months' interest:

$$\$27.08 + \$25.71 + \$24.33 + \$22.93 +$$
$$\$21.51 + \$20.08 = \$141.64$$

Percentage of finance charge paid in first six months:

$$\frac{\$141.64}{\$256.16} \approx 0.5342 = 53.42\%$$

Page 40

$\text{Interest} = (\$1222.08)(0.15)\left(\frac{1}{12}\right) \approx \$15.28$

$\text{Balance due} = \$1222.08 + \$15.28 = \$1237.36$

SECTION 3

Page 57

To find the amount financed, we proceed as follows:

$14,500.00	base price
675.00	price of options
495.00	destination charge
940.20	sales tax
40.00	closing cost
+ 50.00	license and registration fee
$16,700.20	total
− 2,200.20	down payment
$14,500.00	amount financed

The monthly payment on this amount for 60 months with $R = 0.07$ is

$$M = P\left[\frac{\frac{R}{12}}{1 - \left(\frac{1}{\frac{R}{12} + 1}\right)^N}\right]$$

$$= (\$14{,}500.00)\left[\frac{\frac{0.07}{12}}{1 - \left(\frac{1}{\frac{0.07}{12} + 1}\right)^{60}}\right]$$

$$\approx \$287.12.$$

The total payment for the loan is

$$A = NM = 60(\$287.12) = \$17{,}227.20.$$

The total cost of the car is

$17,227.20	total loan payment
+ 2200.20	down payment
$19,427.40	total cost of car

Page 60

From Table 10, we can see that a loan of $13,000.00 for 36 months at 6% corresponds to a monthly payment of $395.49.

Page 62

For a down payment of $2000.00, the amount financed is $10,618.75. Therefore,

$$M = P\left[\frac{\frac{R}{12}}{1 - \left(\frac{1}{\frac{R}{12} + 1}\right)^N}\right]$$

$$= (\$10,618.75)\left[\frac{\frac{0.06}{12}}{1 - \left(\frac{1}{\frac{0.06}{12} + 1}\right)^{48}}\right]$$

$$\approx \$249.38.$$

Total payments $= 48(\$249.38) = \$11,970.24$

Total cost of car $=$ total payments $+$ downpayment $+$ trade allowance

$$= \$11,970.24 + \$2000.00 + \$3200.00$$

$$= \$17,170.24$$

Page 64

To find the balance due, we let $P = \$15,000.00$, $R = 0.05$, $M = \$283.07$, and $n = 36$.
The balance due after 36 payments is

$$B = \left(1 + \frac{R}{12}\right)^n\left(P - \frac{12M}{R}\right) + \frac{12M}{R}$$

$$= \left(1 + \frac{0.05}{12}\right)^{36}\left(\$15,000.00 - \frac{12(\$283.07)}{0.05}\right) + \frac{12(\$283.07)}{0.05}$$

$$\approx \$6452.18.$$

Thus, the balance due on the loan is $6452.18 and the trade-in allowance of $6400.00 is not quite enough to pay off the loan.

SECTION 4

Page 77

The monthly payment is $513.64 (from Table 11). In this case, we have

$N = 12(30) = 360$ and the total payment is $A = 360(\$513.64) = \$184,910.40$.

Therefore, the finance charge is

$$F = A - P = \$184,910.40 - \$70,000.00 = \$114,910.40.$$

Page 80

Minimum monthly payment is $I = (\$75,970.00)(0.09)\left(\frac{1}{12}\right) \approx \$569.78$. For a 25-year term, the monthly payment would be

$$M = (\$75,970.00)\left[\frac{\frac{0.09}{12}}{1 - \left(\frac{1}{\frac{0.09}{12} + 1}\right)^{300}}\right] \approx \$637.54.$$

Page 83

The amount toward interest for the first payment is given by

$$I = PRT = (\$75,000.00)(0.0825)\left(\frac{1}{12}\right) \approx \$515.63.$$

Since the payment is $563.45, the amount toward principal for the first month is given by

$563.45	monthly payment
+ 515.63	interest payment
$47.82	principal payment

Thus, the balance after the first payment is

$75,000.00	balance before first payment
− 47.82	principal payment
$74,952.18	balance after first payment

Continuing the process for 12 payments gives us the following schedule. (cont.)

Payment Number	Balance Before Payment	Payment	Interest Payment	Principal Payment	Balance After Payment
1	$75,000.00	$563.45	$515.63	$47.82	$74,952.18
2	$74,952.18	$563.45	$515.30	$48.15	$74,904.03
3	$74,904.03	$563.45	$514.97	$48.48	$74,855.55
4	$74,855.55	$563.45	$514.63	$48.82	$74,806.73
5	$74,806.73	$563.45	$514.30	$49.15	$74,757.58
6	$74,757.58	$563.45	$513.96	$49.49	$74,708.09
7	$74,708.09	$563.45	$513.62	$49.83	$74,658.26
8	$74,658.26	$563.45	$513.28	$50.17	$74,608.09
9	$74,608.09	$563.45	$512.93	$50.52	$74,557.57
10	$74,557.57	$563.45	$512.58	$50.87	$74,506.70
11	$74,506.70	$563.45	$512.23	$51.22	$74,455.48
12	$74,455.48	$563.45	$511.88	$51.57	$74,403.91

The total payment during the first year is 12($563.45) = $6761.40. By adding the interest column, we see that the total paid toward interest in the first year is $6165.31 and by adding the principal column we see that the total paid toward principal is $596.09. Thus, the percentage of the first year's payments which goes toward interest is

$$\frac{\$6165.31}{\$6761.40} \approx 91.18\%$$

and the percentage toward principal is

$$\frac{\$596.09}{\$6761.40} \approx 8.82\%.$$

Page 86

Robin and Thomas made a total payment of $563.24 + $440.05 = $1003.29. Of this amount, $525.00 goes toward interest. Therefore, the amount applied toward the principal is $1003.29 − $525.00 = $478.29.

a. Thus, the balance after this payment is
   balance = $70,000.00 − $478.29 = $69,521.71.

b. To find the amount of interest the Clarkes saved by making this additional payment, we observe from the amortization schedule that Robin and Thomas would not have reached a balance of approximately $69,521.71 until their 12th regular payment. This represents an eventual savings of $5755.57.

Page 89

We begin by finding the balance after 60 payments.

$$B = \left(1 + \frac{0.085}{12}\right)^{60}\left(\$66,500.00 - \frac{12(\$511.33)}{0.085}\right) + \frac{12(\$511.33)}{0.085} \approx \$63,500.84$$

The equity is

$85,000.00	selling price of home
- 63,500.84	balance due on mortgage
$21,499.16	equity

SECTION 5

Page 107

a. Susan's charges since the last billing date total $159.95.

b. If Susan does not pay the $159.95 by May 10, her past
due balance will be $159.95 and she will be assessed a finance charge of

$$F = PRT = (\$159.95)(0.18)\left(\tfrac{1}{12}\right)$$

$$= (\$159.95)(0.015)$$

$$\approx \$2.40.$$

Page 111

We begin by constructing a record of Bob's daily balance as shown in the table.

Date	Purchase	Payment toward Purchase	Payment toward Finance Charge	Purchase Balance	Number of Days
1/9	—	—	—	$360.49	2
1/11	$45.60	—	—	$406.09	5
1/16	—	$244.59	$5.41	$161.50	20
2/5	$175.29	—	—	$336.79	4
			Days in Billing Period =		31

Note that only $244.59 of Bob's payment is applied toward the purchase balance; the remaining $5.41 is used to cover the previous month's finance charge.

a. Now, we can use the table to find the average daily balance:

$$ADB = \frac{2(\$360.49) + 5(\$406.09) + 20(\$161.50) + 4(\$336.79)}{31}$$

$$\approx \$236.41.$$

b. The finance charge is

$$F = (\text{Average Daily Balance})(\text{Monthly Rate})$$

$$= (\$236.41)(0.015)$$

$$\approx \$3.55.$$

Page 113

The unpaid balance on next month's statement is

$254.94   previous balance
−254.49   payment
$0.45   unpaid balance

Since the account has an unpaid balance, the finance charge is based on the average daily balance (without the benefit of a one month grace period). Since the 45¢ is already accounted for in the average daily balance, the finance charge is

$$F = \text{(Average Daily Balance)(Monthly Rate)}$$

$$= (\$235.75)(0.015)$$

$$\approx \$3.54.$$

Note that if Bob and Lynne had left no unpaid balance, the finance charge would have been zero. Thus, the 45¢ error cost $3.54.

Page 115

During this billing period, Judy's account had the balances shown below.

Date	Cash Advance	Balance	Number of Days
8/28	—	—	4
9/1	$400.00	$400.00	9
9/10	$300.00	$700.00	17
		Days in Billing Period =	30

Thus, the average daily balance is

$$ADB = \frac{4(\$0.00) + 9(\$400.00) + 17(\$700.00)}{30}$$

$$\approx \$516.67$$

and the finance charge is

$$F = (\$516.67)(0.0125) = \$6.46.$$

Page 117

Continuing the table from Example 5, we get

Payment Number	Finance Charge	Balance before Payment	Payment	Balance after Payment
1	—— *	$450.00	$22.50	$427.50
2	$5.34	$432.84	$21.64	$411.20
3	$5.14	$416.34	$20.82	$395.52
4	$4.94	$400.46	$20.02	$380.44
5	$4.76	$385.20	$19.26	$365.94
6	$4.57	$370.51	$18.53	$351.98
7	$4.40	$356.38	$17.82	$338.56
8	$4.23	$342.79	$17.14	$325.65
9	$4.07	$329.72	$329.72	$0.00

Total: $37.45

*One month grace period

Since he has now paid $37.45 in finance charges rather than the $24.75 in Example 5, the amount of additional finance charge is

$$\$37.45 - \$24.75 = \$12.70.$$

Page 120

The bank paid out $146.02 on September 20 and received

$$\$149.00 + \$1.30 = \$150.30$$

on November 5. This means that the bank received

$$\$150.30 - \$146.02 = \$4.28$$

in interest for a 46-day loan of $146.02. The annual percentage rate for such a loan is

$$R = \frac{\$4.28}{(\$146.02)\left(\frac{46}{365}\right)} \approx 0.2326 = 23.26\%.$$

Note that if Carla had paid her account on October 15, the bank would have received $4.28 interest for a 25-day loan of $146.02. The annual percentage rate in this case would be

$$R = \frac{\$4.28}{(\$146.02)\left(\frac{25}{365}\right)} \approx 0.4279 = 42.79\%.$$

Answers to Odd-Numbered Exercises

SECTION 1 (pages 1-26)

1.

Date of Loan	Term	Date Due
July 19, 1995	3 months	October 19, 1995
July 19, 1995	90 days	October 17, 1995
May 20, 1996	6 months	November 20, 1996
May 24, 1996	180 days	November 20, 1996
January 13, 1995	18 months	July 13, 1996
January 13, 1996	90 days	April 12, 1996

3. Tax: $29.34, Loan Proceeds: $443.34

5. **a.** $8.87 **b.** $452.21 **c.** $13.38 **d.** $22.25

7. $835.51

9. $836.30

11. $2180.16

13. 18.00%

15. $23.31

17. **a.** $68.18 **b.** 13.6%

19. F: $30.73, R: 15.6%

21. F: $250.00, R: 10.1%

SECTION 2 (pages 27–54)

1. **a.** $138.95
   b. $1667.40
   c. $167.40

3. **a.** $202.85
   b. $36,513.00
   c. $16,513.00

5. **a.** If $N = 6, M = $173.54
   b. If $N = 12, M = $89.79
   c. If $N = 18, M = $61.92
   d. If $N = 24, M = $48.01
   e. If $N = 30, M = $39.70
   Sally should request a term of 24 months.

7. Term should be 18 months. Finance charge for 24 months: $152.24

Finance charge for 18 months: $114.56, Savings: $37.68

9. $86.15

11. First principal payment: $81.36

Balance after first pament: $418.64

13.

Payment Number	Balance before Payment	Payment	Interest Payment	Principal Payment	Balance after Payment
1	$500.00	$86.15	$4.79	$81.36	$418.64
2	$418.64	$86.15	$4.01	$82.14	$336.50
3	$336.50	$86.15	$3.22	$82.93	$253.57
4	$253.57	$86.15	$2.43	$83.72	$169.86
5	$169.85	$86.15	$1.63	$84.52	$85.33
6	$85.33	$86.15	$0.82	$85.33	$0.00

15. 52.1%

17. $256.00

19.

	12 month	18 month
a.	$M = \$81.66$	$M = \$56.57$
b.	$79.92	$F = \$118.26$

For the loan with a greater number of payments (18 months), the monthly payment is less. For the loan with fewer number of payments(12 months), the finance charge is less.

21.

Payment Number	Balance before Payment	Payment	Interest Payment	Principal Payment	Balance after Payment
1	$1200.00	$139.23	$10.50	$128.73	$1071.27
2	$1071.27	$139.23	$9.37	$129.86	$941.41
3	$941.41	$139.23	$8.24	$130.99	$810.42
4	$810.42	$139.23	$7.09	$132.14	$678.28
5	$678.28	$139.23	$5.93	$133.30	$544.98
6	$544.98	$139.23	$4.77	$134.46	$410.52
7	$410.52	$139.23	$3.59	$135.64	$274.88
8	$274.88	$139.23	$2.41	$136.82	$138.06
9	$138.06	$139.27*	$1.21	$138.06	$0.00

*Difference in final payment due to rounding.

23. *24-month plan*: $M = \$96.03$, $F = \$304.72$

18-month plan: $M = \$125.71$, $F = \$262.78$

Finance charge is less for 18 month plan. This is the one she should choose..

SECTION 3 (pages 55–73)

1. $9291.54 amount financed

3. $M \approx \$456.33.$ $\quad F = \$1426.80$

5. $M \approx \$359.19.$ $\quad F = \$2241.12$

7. $14,000.00

9. a. $P = \$9295.00$

$\quad M \approx \$226.92.$ $\quad F = \$1597.16$

b. $P = \$7495.00$

$\quad M \approx \$234.87.$ $\quad F = \$960.32$

11. $B \approx \$8158.60$

13.

n	Balance due after n payments	Total of first n payments	Principal paid after n payments	Interest paid after n payments
6	$12,683.23	$2,737.98	$2,316.77	$421.21
12	$10,296.08	$5,475.96	$4,703.92	$772.04
18	$7,836.42	$8,213.94	$7,163.58	$1,050.36
24	$5,302.03	$10,951.92	$9,697.97	$1,253.95
30	$2,690.66	$13,689.90	$12,309.34	$1,380.56
36	$0.00	$16,427.84	$15,000.00	$1,427.84
36*	-$0.04	$16,427.84	$15,000.04	$1,427.84

*These are numbers that are possible when using the balance due formula without taking into consideration the rounding error adjustment in the final payment. There is a $0.04 error due to rounding that would be deducted from the final payment as an adjustment, resulting in the values that are shown in the row immediately preceding this one.

15. $M \approx \$365.48.$ $\quad F = \$771.52$ (two years)

$\quad M \approx \$199.08.$ $\quad F = \$1555.84$ (four years)

Savings in finance charges: $784.32

SECTION 4 (pages 75–104)

1. $71,875.00

3. From Table 11

   a. $M = \$585.51$, Total Payment $= \$140,522.40$
     $F = \$70,522.40$

   b. $M = \$540.27$, Total Payment $= \$162,081.00$
     $F = \$92,081.00$

   c. $M = \$513.64$, Total Payment $= \$184,910.40$
     $F = \$114,910.40$

   d. $M = \$497.18$, Total Payment $= \$208,815.60$
     $F = \$138,815.60$

5. a. percent decrease in payment $\approx 7.7\%$

    percent increase in finance charge $\approx 30.6\%$

  b. percent decrease in payment $\approx 12.3\%$

    percent increase in finance charge $\approx 62.9\%$

  c. percent decrease in payment $\approx 15.1\%$

    percent increase in finance charge $\approx 96.8\%$

7. $I = \$525.00$

9. From Table 11, $M = \$617.45$. The balance after n payments is given by

$$B = \left(1 + \frac{0.08}{12}\right)^n\left(\$80,000.00 - \frac{12(\$617.45)}{0.08}\right) + \frac{12(\$617.45)}{0.08}$$

Time in Years	n	Balance Due After n Payments	Total of First n Payments	Principal Paid After n Payments	Interst Paid After n Payments
5	60	$73,819.37	$37,047.00	$6,180.63	$30,866.37
10	120	$64,611.19	$74,094.00	$1,5388.81	$58,705.19
15	180	$50,892.42	$111,141.00	$2,9107.58	$82,033.42
20	240	$30,453.57	$148,188.00	$4,9546.43	$98,641.57
25	300	$0.00*	$185,235.00	$80,000.00	$105,235.00

*Adjustment of an additional $2.83 on the 300th payment due to rounding.

11. $M \approx \$611.59$

Pmt. No.	Balance Before Payment	Payment	Interest Payment	Principal Payment	Balance After Payment
43	$67,152.10	$611.59	$531.62	$79.97	$67,072.13
44	$67,072.13	$611.59	$530.99	$80.60	$66,991.53
45	$66,991.53	$611.59	$530.35	$81.24	$66,910.29
46	$66,910.29	$611.59	$529.71	$81.88	$66,828.41
47	$66,828.41	$611.59	$529.06	$82.53	$66,745.88
48	$66,745.88	$611.59	$528.40	$83.19	$66,662.69

13. The extra payment of $409.44 would all go to reduce the principal and would give a balance after payment of $66,662.69. Thus, she would save the interest of payments 44 through 48. Interest saved is $2648.51.

15. $M \approx \$457.37$

Balance after 12 payments $\approx \$49,749.74$

Principal paid after 12 payments $= \$250.26$
Total of first 12 payments $= \$5488.44$
Interest paid after 12 months $= \$5238.18$

Percentage paid toward interest $\approx 95.4\%$

Percentage paid toward principal $\approx 4.6\%$

17. $M \approx \$742.27$

$B \approx \$44,424.27$

Equity $= \$28,483.18$

SECTION 5 (pages 105–130)

1. $ADB = \$107.80$

3. $ADB \approx \$256.01$

5. **a.** $F \approx \$2.14$

   b. $F \approx \$2.56$

7. **a.** $F \approx \$1.70$

   b. $F \approx \$4.59$

   c. $F \approx \$10.48$

   d. $F \approx \$19.29$

9. $ADB = \$230.00$

   $F \approx \$2.88$

11. **a.** Balance = $\$146.30$
       $F \approx \$1.83$

    b. New Balance = $\$148.13$

13.

Payment Number	Finance Charge	Balance before Payment	Payment	Balance after Payment
1	—	$750.00	$75.00	$675.00
2	$8.44	$683.44	$68.34	$615.10
3	$7.69	$622.79	$62.28	$560.51
4	$7.01	$567.52	$56.75	$510.77
5	$6.38	$517.15	$51.72	$465.43

15. $349.68

17. $F = \$18.95$

    $R \approx 101.1\%$

SECTION 6 (pages 131–138)

1. $F \approx \$46.40$

$R \approx 0.2216 = 22.16\%$

3. $F = \$112.50$

$R = 0.09125 \approx 9.13\%$

5.

$14,659.00	base price
215.00	cruise control
435.00	leather interior
189.00	rear window defroster
+ 395.00	destination charge
$15,893.00	total
−5,600.00	trade-in allowance
$9709.00	taxable amount
+ 617.58	sales tax
$10,910.58	
− 2,000.00	down payment
$$8,910.58	amount financed

7. From Table 10, the monthly payment for $12,000.00 at 7% for four years is $287.35. Therefore,

$B \approx \$6418.23$

9. $M \approx \$523.41$

$B \approx \$57,688.55$

Equity $= \$7311.45$